Napper

Through A Glass Darkly

Alan Jackaman

 WATERSIDE PRESS

Napper: Through A Glass Darkly
Alan Jackaman

ISBN 978-1-909976-70-2 (Paperback)
ISBN 978-1-910979-85-3 (Epub ebook)
ISBN 978-1-910979-86-0 (Adobe ebook)

Cover design © 2019 Waterside Press by www.gibgob.com.

Main UK distributor Gardners Books, 1 Whittle Drive, Eastbourne, East Sussex, BN23 6QH. Tel: +44 (0)1323 521777; sales@gardners.com; www.gardners.com

North American distribution Ingram Book Company, One Ingram Blvd, La Vergne, TN 37086, USA. Tel: (+1) 615 793 5000; inquiry@ingramcontent.com

Cataloguing-In-Publication Data A catalogue record for this book can be obtained from the British Library.

Ebook *Napper: Through A Glass Darkly* is available as an ebook and to subscribers of Ebrary, Ebsco, Myilibrary and Dawsonera.

Published 2019 by
Waterside Press Ltd
Sherfield Gables, Sherfield on Loddon,
Hook, Hampshire, RG27 0JG.

Online catalogue WatersidePress.co.uk

Table of Contents

About the author

Alan Jackaman spent over a quarter of a century as a police officer, mostly with the CID investigating murder. Born in Bury St Edmunds he joined the Royal Navy in 1966 serving in frigates for the next ten years from Aden to the South China sea, Singapore and the West Indies, during which time he qualified as a diver. After completing military service in 1976, he joined Suffolk Constabulary where he first experienced murder investigation.

In 1979 Alan Jackaman transferred to the Metropolitan Police Service, serving initially at Notting Hill. Appointed detective constable and posted to Clapham, he was made exhibits officer in the double murder of two drug-dealers. This led to his involvement in many other murder cases, some high profile. Selected as part of the first ever MPS dedicated Murder Investigation Team in 1994, he continued investigating murders until his retirement from active police work in 2002 by when he had received a commendation for his work in bringing Robert Napper to justice. He then joined the newly formed Murder Review Group, examining cold cases and advising on unsolved murders in London and nationwide.

In his spare time he enjoys sailing and is a qualified ocean yacht master. He is also a keen distance runner, skier and motorcyclist.

Publisher's Note

The views and opinions expressed in this book are those of the author entirely by whom they are honestly held. Readers should draw their own conclusions about any claims made or facts and opinions stated or reproduced, concerning which the possibility of alternative perspectives, narratives, descriptions and interpretations should be borne in mind.

Acknowledgements

This book could not have been written without the help and memories of colleagues who worked with me during the critical phases of the investigation.

Special mention goes to Roger Boydell-Smith.

Also to the friendship and support of Jack Morrison.

This book is dedicated to the memory of Samantha and Jazmine Bisset, who, although never met in life will always remain in my heart.

Illustrations

Introduction

This book was written to record for history the tragic circumstances which led to one man committing a sequence of vicious sexual assaults through to the murders of Rachel Nickell and Samantha and Jazmine Bisset. It has taken Alan Jackaman over 25 years to come to terms with what happened and he is now ready to relate his part in the downfall and imprisonment of Robert Napper.

The book, which contains a good deal of information not until now in the public domain, encompasses many intriguing aspects of the police investigations. In addition to a straightforward account of the solving of a heinous and complex series of crimes, it delves into media fascination with serious crime and demonstrates how the press may "latch on" to one murder whilst ignoring another, even more horrific one. It questions the strategic reasoning behind how the hierarchy of the police can be influenced by the intensity of media pressure as seen in the imbalance of financial support between the high profile Nickell investigation on Wimbledon Common and less public, more locally reported, Bisset enquiry.

The underlying reasons why Robert Napper became the psychotic killer he did are examined, from his troubled childhood to minor offending, progressing to serious sexual assaults, rapes and culminating in three brutal murders. It also looks at the emergence of modern criminal profiling in police investigations and its shortcomings.

The author has the benefit of having been appointed as an investigator on the Bisset case from the day of the murder through to seeing the case linked first to the Green Chain Walk series of rapes and (following Napper's conviction for the Bisset murders), the unearthing of evidence to prove that the same man also killed Rachel Nickell.

Like the Bisset case in Plumstead, south east London, the murder of Rachel in south west London had become a "sticker", following the early but misguided arrest and public vilification of the wrong man, Colin

Stagg, an enticingly convenient "oddball" (who ultimately secured substantial damages against the Metropolitan Police Service). Until Alan's team of detectives became insistent, no-one had connected the two sets of tragic events or linked them to the Green Chain Walk rapes and, as the book shows, sheer persistence is what at times kept that possible connection alive. The book shows how Alan Jackaman's (and his colleagues') determination ensured this even when faced with the disbelief of other officers and taunts such as, "It was Napper wot done it." But Alan's deep concern for Samantha, Jazmine and their family together with the terrible circumstances of their deaths and similarities with the Nickell case just would not allow him to let go.

Unusually, the story is laid out from the point of view of an officer of junior rank. Alan was simply a detective constable until given the (initially) temporary rank of detective sergeant for the purposes of the Bisset investigation. As a result, he is perhaps less inhibited than some higher in the police hierarchy when describing the problems which arise from "investigating on the cheap" or telling of the dramatic twists and turns of what seemed, in the Bisset case, to be the killing of an obscure mother and child in an unfashionable district of London. In contrast, the Nickell case, in the full glare of publicity, attracted major funding and the application of innovative (though what proved to be questionable) investigative techniques. The pressures on all three teams were enormous but the Bisset case and Green Chain Walk rapes were always poor cousins of the media-obsessed Wimbledon case.

The book follows the murder and rape cases from the start of each to the solving of a series of the twentieth century's most notorious crimes and conviction of one of the UK's most dangerous ever killers. It also looks into the dark mind of Robert Napper, his bizarre behaviour, delusions, family history, strange "doodles" and the sheer "luck" that allowed him to remain free to continue his offending for so long.

CHAPTER 1

"Take him down!"

Alan walked out of St Paul's underground and turned left toward the Central Criminal Court, more popularly known as the Old Bailey. The December weather was cool but clear, the date the 18th December 2008. He felt empty-handed with no court papers to carry, no briefcase, a feeling as if he had forgotten something stayed with him as he strode at an even pace. There was no hurry, the appearance time in court was set for 10.30 am and, he was, as usual, too early.

The vast edifice of St Paul's Cathedral loomed on the opposite side of the road, although there were the usual throngs of people on the street the vast rush to work was well past. He felt calm, today the fear was absent of not knowing what to expect in the cockpit of the criminal court, no queasy feeling in the pit of his stomach, only a sense of an ending.

Turning left into Old Bailey, so called because it once formed the fortified boundary walls of the old city, he could see the press were ahead of him, already gathering at the main entrance to the court, their cameras at the ready, reporters voicing their preliminary openings into hungry lenses. He walked past the jostling film crews, unrecognised, towards the familiar entrance. Things here had changed considerably since the last time this particular case had caused his presence to be summoned to the cradle of justice. Now it was akin to boarding an aeroplane. Bag screens, security guards, interrogations. Alan joined the queue, showed his Home Office identity card and was filtered through. At the first trial 13 years before in 1995, he had pushed open the double doors, waved his warrant card at a disinterested member of the court staff and that was that.

Eventually he was through to the main area of the court building. This was far more familiar territory. A cavernous, marbled hallway with statues lining its sides. Courtrooms led off on the right hand side, Courts 7 and 8, Court 19. All playing out their tragedies. Alan thought to himself how often he had been to this building, now it was probably his last time. He knew where he was headed, to the far end, No. 1 Court. The most infamous, but, oddly, one of the smallest courtrooms.

A crowd had already gathered around the heavy wooden benches near to the entrance of the court. A hub-bub of conversation interspersed with laughter. High above them inscribed into the wall unnoticed and embossed in gold-leaf, the statement:

"Defend the children of the poor.
And punish the wrongdoer."

The irony of this pronouncement always brought a wry smile to Alan's face. "So long as you have the money," he thought.

He saw Roger Boydell-Smith standing deep in conversation with one of the detectives of the investigating team. Roger was instantly recognisable, shaven head, tall, easy smile, his charm enhanced by a not forgotten Lancashire burr. Roger broke off his conversation and walked over.

"Morning Al, bit of a circus here today."

"I hope we're going to get in. The world and his dog have turned-up."

"Don't worry, I've been given these by the SIO."

Roger handed Alan a small piece of paper with his name on it and a short printed authorisation to enter the courtroom.

Alan scanned his eyes over the slip. "Very good of them," he said, unable to keep the sarcasm out of his voice. "I think Rog, we had better get in while we can, we don't want to miss this."

Roger was coming to the end of his service as a detective in the Metropolitan Police Service. A bright, easy going man, Alan had first worked with him when they had both been seconded to the investigation of the murder of Samantha Bisset and her daughter Jazmine. Roger had been appointed as exhibits officer. They had worked together daily for nearly two years on that case and, subsequent to that, had remained friends and taken an interest in the ongoing life of Robert Napper. The man they were here today to see.

They entered the double swing doors, the brass plate gleaming with its bold lettering: "Court 1." An usher studied their passes and directed them to seats at the rear. Behind the expansive doors the courtroom was surprisingly small but what it lacked in size it more than made up for in atmosphere. In this room the famous and the infamous had been examined and cross-examined, their lives in the balance, from Dr Crippen to Reginald and Ronald Kray. They had risen from the cells below, up the narrow staircase and into the defendant's box, known as the dock, to plead their cases. Many were to retrace their steps one last time to take their places in the condemned cell.

Roger and Alan each took their seats in the rapidly filling courtroom. Bewigged barristers chatted together on the benches below. The judge's bench, high at the rear, stood empty. A buzz of excitement was in the air. This was going to be an extraordinary moment. Alan looked across the courtroom; he recognised a few of the faces but most were unknown to him. Thirteen years had passed since the first trial, which had been in the same place and was an affair of much lower profile and of little public interest. Indeed he had been surprised today's case was listed for No. 1 Court. Probably some last minute shuffling of available venues.

No chat passed between Alan and Roger. The business of the judiciary went on around them, oblivious to their part in the drama. Time ticked on until suddenly the blue of a prison officer's uniform popped-up into the dock, a hush fell over the courtroom and eyes turned in the officer's direction. A moment later Alan could see the back of the man he instantly recognised even though the man's face was turned away from him looking towards the judge's bench. Wearing an open-neck, checked shirt, his hair was thinning, but still parted schoolboy style. His long neck still carried the scars of childhood acne. His name was Robert Clive Napper.

Moments later an usher intoned, "Silence in court. Stand." A brief shuffling of papers and backsides off seats, then as demanded … silence. The red-robed judge, Mr Justice Griffith Williams took his place on the high dais and sat down, the rest of those in court followed suit. The prisoner was asked to stand. Alan was now able to get a much clearer view of him as Napper rose to his feet and looked straight ahead at the judge. As the charges were read, Napper looked slowly right and left as if searching for someone in the arena before him. Alan had a clear view of his profile, the slightly protruding teeth over a weak chin and thought how prison life must suit him, he had hardly aged.

The words of the clerk droned on. Alan was having difficulty concentrating, the event was so overwhelming.

"…Murder… Rachel Nickell on…" A clarification was made on the plea. Napper would plead not guilty to murder but guilty to manslaughter by reason of diminished responsibility, then the briefest of pauses.

"And how do you plead?"

A longer pause, then almost inaudibly, in a voice which stumbled slightly over the one word, Napper replied, "Guilty."

There was no commotion; the court remained quiet.

David Fisher for the defence made a few comments in which he conveyed Napper's apology to Rachel's partner, her son Alex, her parents and her close friends for the "dreadful things he did."

Napper also wanted to apologise to a certain Colin Stagg.

The judge made his comments. Then he ordered that Napper be returned to Broadmoor Special Hospital and informed him there was little prospect of him ever being released.

Then, the fateful words, "Take him down!"

Napper turned 180 degrees to face the steps. His watery blue eyes stared ahead and for a moment focussed on Alan. There was instant recognition as they held each other's gaze, Napper hesitated momentarily, his pale blue eyes fixed, a slight smile ghosted onto his lips.

Alan mouthed the words, "Hello Rob."

Urged on by the prison officer, Napper disappeared down the steps.

CHAPTER 2

The Start

O n receiving his instructions to attend at Thamesmead Police Station on the morning of Thursday 4th November 1993, Alan thought little of it. The case he had been working on was drawing to close, a gangland revenge job in south London. The least interesting of all murder investigations, and generally the hardest work when it came to persuading witnesses to come forward. His detective inspector had told him to report to Thamesmead.

"Sounds like a domestic," he had said, as if intimating this was the bottom of the pile for murder investigation. Alan didn't mind, anything to get away from the brain-numbing tedium of his current role at Camberwell. He wondered where Thamesmead Police Station was and headed in the general direction of the new high rise estate in south London. Locating it on the map was easier than finding it in reality. Eventually, after driving fruitlessly around the wide, high rise flanked roads in his battered, brown Fiesta, he saw what he was looking for. Set back from the main road, behind a ten foot wire fence, a group of grey prefabs clustered around a blue, MPS notice board. The board, apart from one forlorn leaflet, extolling the virtues of a career in the police, was empty. It was an old building, but not in years. Old police stations, many of which were built around the turn of the nineteenth century of red brick, all to a standard pattern, have a welcoming air, a severe charm seeping from their smog blackened bricks.

Thamesmead Police Station was about as welcoming as a car crash and equally as shocking in its blunt dilapidated façade. No lost property or dog would be readily handed in here. He drove through the open gate which was pinned back with a rusty fire extinguisher and parked his car among several others in the adjoining car park. It was starting to drizzle as he walked across the uneven tarmac. Wearing a threadbare grey suit, the attire worn by most detectives, he nevertheless felt overdressed in the landscape of grime. He entered the unwelcoming public front office. A uniformed officer stood behind the desk, which more resembled a barrier than a place to greet and assist the public. Alan thought fleetingly, "No wonder they call it a 'jump'."

He flashed his warrant card and the constable unbolted and lifted the flap pointing vaguely towards the only door. Walking through it and within ten feet, Alan found himself in the incident room where the usual organized chaos was underway. Detective Sergeant Bob Thomas was clearing an area from which he could command the office. Alan introduced himself as Bob tore his eyes from the mounting paperwork.

"Hello. Write your name up on the board will you?"

He pointed to one of three large white boards fixed to the wall, Alan added his name to the seven already appended. Next to Bob his indexers, Enid Lamb, Pam Robinson and Jane Stutchbury beavered away, constructing in-trays for messages, statements and all other forms of paper communication. In the centre of the largest desk was a big steel wheel known as a carousel. The wheel was divided into sections kept apart with headlined index cards. Enid was telling Pam, "I think this should have gone on HOLMES, don't you?"

HOLMES (Home Office Large Major Enquiry System) was the established computer system used in complex murder enquiries. It had been introduced after the enquiry team on the Yorkshire Ripper investigation had lost track of valuable information because of the vast, cross-county nature of the enquiry. It was standard practice by now to use it but was left to the senior investigating officer's (SIO's) discretion. Pam, laughing replied, "I don't think Mr Banks will be using a computer if he can help it."

Looking-up Alan could see the entrance to an offshoot office; he made his way toward the open doorway. Behind the desk in the tiny room sat Detective Inspector Bryan Reeve, his ear glued to a telephone with his free hand shuffling paperwork. Bryan looked-up, stared at Alan and raised his eyebrows quizzically whilst still shouting into the telephone.

Bryan was more than a little hard of hearing. His hand rose up from the desk and made a beckoning motion for Alan to fully enter the office. A difference of about six inches.

"Right, get on with it then," Bryan bellowed into the phone, followed by a slamming down of the handpiece into its careworn cradle. Alan introduced himself.

"Hello Al." No formality here then thought Alan, with more than a little relief. "You will be on the outside team," Bryan continued, "Get yourself down to the scene at Winns Common, Roger Boydell-Smith is down there doing exhibits, he will bring you up to speed. Full briefing here 5 pm by Micky Banks."

The telephone rang again. Alan backed out of the door, it was easier than a three point turn. Back in the main office, phones were chiming their persistent call and work progressed with the standard setting-up of an incident room. As he passed Bob Thomas, Alan ventured, "I thought it was a domestic?" Bob looked-up from his burgeoning empire. "That's what we all thought, the boyfriend, er..." He glanced at a white board. "Cosy, was nicked this morning by night duty CID. We are not so sure now."

"The DI has sent me to the scene," Alan said.

Bob Thomas' attention was already somewhere else. "Okay, see you back here at 5 o'clock for the briefing."

Alan was relieved to see his Fiesta had retained its wheels and sat in the driving seat, he took out his even more battered *London A to Z* and looked-up the address he had jotted down from the white board: 1a Heathfield Terrace. He slammed the creaky car door shut and drove the two miles or so to Winns Common, Plumstead. Driving up Kings Highway, Alan was struck by how rural it seemed. Dense woodland on the right petered out into open common.

The murder scene was easy to see on the left. Set back from the main road, several police cars were parked outside the end of a terrace in a cul-de-sac. The three storey terraced row of 1960s houses looked directly out onto Winns Common over the cul-de-sac and main road.

Parking his car 50 or so yards from the scene Alan took in the surroundings. The weather was turning cold, he grabbed his coat, it had rained and felt like it was going to do so again, dark clouds gathered ominously over the common. Heathfield Terrace was purpose built to be divided into flats. Walking past the steps which led down to the front entrance of No. 1a, he noted that the whole block stood isolated. To the rear was a green patch stretching down 25 yards to an iron railed fence standing about four feet high, no real barrier. The front of the building faced out directly onto the pavement and all entrances to the flats were to be made here, with the exception of 1a which had its entrance on the side of the building at the foot of a flight of stone steps.

The flat was cordoned off at the top of the steps. He gave his name to the constable manning the cordon who entered it dutifully into the visitor's log. The front door was ajar. Alan didn't enter. He could see within the flat someone was employed with a video camera, going from room-to-room, performing a commentary as they went. The camera-man approached the front door and Alan could see blood on the floor in the hallway, a lot of blood. Space was very limited so Alan stayed at the threshold. He could see the blood trailed away from the large pool next to the front door towards what was the living-room at the end of the hallway.

Alan recognised Roger. They had met, but never worked together before. Roger was standing next to the entrance to the living-room door just 20 feet or so along the hallway. Alan called out and Roger looked-up and made his way toward him. They shook hands, Roger wearing thin rubber gloves.

"Hello Rog, I have been seconded to the investigation, what's it about?"

"Hello mate, grab yourself a pair of gloves from the box." He indicated a cardboard box by the front door. Alan squeezed into the gloves, the inevitable snap as they rolled out onto his wrists, as Roger said, "Prepare yourself, this is like nothing I have ever seen."

Alan thought to himself that was highly unlikely. It always made him smile when some police officer being interviewed on TV was moved to announce that in 25 years of police service they had never seen anything so horrific. His response was always to murmur at the TV, "You should get out more."

Roger said, "Mind where you step." A route had been marked out to the left of the hallway. Roger stopped by the doorway to a small bedroom, a child's room, flowered wallpaper, toys tidily placed in a box at the foot of a cot. He could just make out the figure of a small child. Her head was the only part of her exposed from the bedclothes. Apparently asleep, until on closer inspection the tell tale blue lips portrayed death.

"Jazmine," said Roger, in a hushed tone as if not to wake her from her slumber. "She is four." Alan look down at the child. The red curls unfurled on the pillow. Roger whispered, "You've seen nothing yet." He led the way out of the room as Alan glanced over his shoulder, half expecting the child to move, the weight of tragedy not yet fully established in his thoughts.

With just enough room they stood together at the entrance to the living-room. Two men were deep in conversation, Dr Ian Hill pathologist and Detective Sergeant Lionel Barclay. Dr Hill seemed in distress. Lying in the centre of the room were the remains, for they could only be described as such, of Samantha Bisset. At first glance she resembled a grotesque puppet. Limbs spread in an awkward pose, the ligaments at her knees had been cut through. She lay on her back, her torso cut open from vulva to throat, ribs cut through, exposing all internal organs which had themselves been horribly disturbed. A cushion had been placed under her buttocks, she was partially clothed in a bra, which had been cut through at the front, a pair of short socks and a bathrobe. Her face with sightless eyes, one blackened, had also been cut, her mouth was fixed slightly open, the face of a young woman. Samantha was 27-years-old.

They looked down upon the prone body in silence. The sound of cars driving past outside, rooks cawing in the woods opposite. Roger said, "We are expecting the undertakers soon, bodies to Greenwich mortuary." The word "bodies" reminded Alan of the dead infant just yards away. It was a lot to take in.

The crime scene photographer, Carol England was clicking away. Because of the confused first reports of the crime the photographic branch had been informed the scene was of a domestic nature. Carol wasn't expecting the one that confronted her, although she was very experienced and had seen and been asked to photograph many a horrific diorama, Carol was totally unprepared for what she was asked to do. It may have been the accumulation of seeing a succession of grizzly sights over the years and this was the final straw. She was later to be unable to account for some missing photographs and could remember very little of what had happened.

Carol seemed to be working in her usual professional manner and then was suddenly overwhelmed. Until that moment no-one present gave her a second thought as she professionally went about her task. In any event she was unable to continue and an ambulance was called to take her away from the scene for a full check-up, unfortunately the experience affected her badly. She became haunted by what she had seen, eventually culminating in her being unable to continue as an MPS photographer. Another photographer was summoned and luckily was able to capture any missing shots.

Alan turned to Roger. "Well Rog, one thing is for sure, this is no domestic."

CHAPTER 3

Scramble

Alan left Roger at Heathfield Crescent. There was no way the scenes of crime team would be finished in time for the briefing, in fact they wouldn't finish until two o'clock the following morning such was the complexity of the extraordinary scene.

Back at Thamesmead a team gathered in the incident room. There was very little spare room for the 15 or so assembled investigators. The carousel was taking shape, gradually filling with index cards. The indexers, Pam, Enid and Jane worked on obliviously amidst the chatter of the assembled team.

At 5 pm a hush settled over the office as the SIO, Detective Superintendent Banks entered. He picked his way through the crush to the end of the room and turned to face the assembly. Micky Banks, famous for his curt manner, humour and vast experience, his craggy face sporting a greying, bristling moustache, acknowledged his deputy, Detective Inspector Bryan Reeve with a nod.

"Thank you Bryan." Lighting a cigarette he turned to the team. "I have here a video-recording taken at the scene." He flipped open his briefcase and withdrew a video cassette which he handed to the office manager Bob Thomas.

"There is only one copy of this video and that is how it's going to stay. I want you all to watch closely. Do not comment until it is finished." He placed the recording into a machine which had been previously set-up. At a nod from Banks, Bob Thomas flicked the switch. A hush fell over the compacted gathering. The video flickered away on a tiny screen. All watched as the camera tracked along from the front door of 1a Heathfield Terrace to the living-room and dwelled over Samantha's body focussing on her injuries. The film then panned around the room and went to Samantha's bedroom, and then to Jazmine's room.

Alan's thoughts kept repeating, "Blue lips, blue lips."

Not a sound was heard, not one expletive and, unusually, no comment of totally inappropriate black humour usually associated with such macabre moments. The little video monitor flickered from room-to-room, in the living-room it concentrating on the body of Samantha, then panned around showing items of clothing strewn haphazardly. As the camera panned, it showed the balcony windows next to Samantha, the rattan blinds were down in the closed position. The camera followed the blood trail into the hallway where further items of clothing were strewn about. Blood smears were clearly visible, travelling from the large blood pool at the front door towards the living-room.

The group watched the tiny screen continue in silence as the camera entered Jazmine's bedroom, nobody stirred. It focussed on the cot and dwelt, firstly on her face and then back to show a sweet child, apparently sleeping in her bed. Alan had seen some sights, an ex-serviceman with ten years experience of conflicts around the globe, and then another 14 years of police work, the greater part in murder investigation. The impact of these events, great and small had flowed over him. No after effects, no flashbacks, shakes, jitters or any thought of recourse to some form of analysis. Something inside him knocked at his heart, from this moment it was now going to be different.

The video film ended. Those who could grab seats shuffled back and grabbed them, those remaining stood at the rear. "There is no other way," said Banks, "of conveying the horror of this murder than to show you all the video film of 1a Heathfield Terrace." He continued his briefing, explaining how the bodies had been found by Samantha's boyfriend Conrad Ellam known as "Cosy", when he returned home from working a night shift in a local factory at 7 am. Cosy did not live full-time with Samantha, Jazmine was not his child, but he was at Samantha's flat more often than not.

Cosy had been surprised when he tried his key to the front door and it wouldn't open. It had been deadlocked from the inside, something which Samantha never did, she was far from being security conscious.

Cosy knocked and shouted without any response. Knowing that Samantha and Jazmine could be nowhere else at that time of day he began to be alarmed. In panic his first thought was to telephone his boss at work. He looked through the letter-box from where he could see clothing strewn along the hallway and a pool of something he could not identify near the front door. Remembering he had a deadlock key he managed to open the door. Calling out, he walked down the hallway. The doorway was open to Jazmine's room, Cosy glanced in but didn't stop. As he entered the living-room he could immediately see Samantha. Still unable to take it all in, he believed for a moment somebody had played some bad practical joke upon him and had left a scarecrow effigy on the floor. Samantha's head at this stage was covered with towelling and her body was splayed out in the attitude of a stringless puppet. The horror began to sink in and Cosy backed from the room, such was his shock he did not even stay to look at Jazmine. He stumbled into the kitchen and, using the telephone on the wall, dialled 999 and asked for the police.

The first police to arrive were the local CID from Plumstead. DC Graham Cooke took charge. Cosy was waiting for him at the entrance to the flat in a very agitated state. DC Cooke noted that Cosy's hands were heavily stained in red. He took a brief look at the scene and arranged for it to be cordoned off and relayed a message to Plumstead Police Station for the murder team to be called. He then arrested Cosy on suspicion for the murders and had him taken to Plumstead Police Station where, after he had explained the facts to the custody officer, he was placed in a cell.

Meanwhile, to add to the ever growing bizarre nature of events, the news of the murder had spread through Plumstead Police Station and reached the ears of a sergeant who was in the process of training three new probationer constables. Without more ado the sergeant grabbed a police car from the station yard and, with a brief explanation to his charges, "This will be a good one for you to see," drove off with them to Heathfield Terrace. Luckily for the unfolding investigation, members of the murder team beat him to the scene and the sergeant and his group were refused entry.

As Micky Banks continued with his briefing, tasks were allocated. "Alan, I want you to contact the parents, they live in Scotland. Arrange

for them to come down, we will need them to identify the body." He
went on by saying one witness had come forward saying she had seen
an unusual vehicle the day before parked near Samantha's address, it was
no longer there and she could not remember ever seeing it before. It was
an old General Post Office (GPO) van in its original, but very faded yellow colours, the GPO sign on the side had been roughly painted over
but was still clearly visible. These types of van had been made by their
thousands and had become popular as makeshift campervans with hippy
communities as cheap, spacious vehicles to travel between communities
and events. The witness had provided a sketch which showed small windows in the sides. Work was already in progress to find out how many
of these vans were still registered and to whom.

House-to-house enquiries were also being progressed. One witness
had heard what she thought were two men arguing loudly in Samantha's flat which was below her. One of the men was shouting, "Leave it
alone." Generally, Samantha kept very much to herself and caused the
neighbours no disturbance.

Banks informed the team that Cosy had been released. There was
nothing to suggest he may have been the killer and the hands steeped
in red were as a result of red dye from his work in the paint factory.
Nobody could be completely ruled out at this stage but Cosy was now
to be treated as a witness. The meeting then devolved into allocating
tasks and dividing teams. The main players had already been appointed,
Detective Sergeant Bob Thomas as office manager, Detective Constable
Roger Boydell-Smith as exhibits officer and Detective Sergeant John Bull
to head the outside investigation team.

The meeting broke up with instructions to carry on the house-to-
house enquiries and obtain witness statements. Alan approached Pam.

"What have we got on mum and dad?"

Pam drew the card from the carousel. It transpired they lived south of
Aberdeen. Jack and Margaret Morrison. Jack was Samantha's stepfather,
her real father Douglas Bisset had worked on newspapers as a journalist
and water colourist, he had died in 1980 when Samantha was 14. Margaret had remarried and the family had moved to Dundee where Jack

owned and ran a building company. Samantha was Margaret's only child. It followed in tragic sequence that Jazmine was her only grandchild.

Alan noted the telephone number and handed the card back to Pam who duly recorded "DC Jackaman appointed family liaison" and placed it carefully back in its position in the wheel. He found the flight times, they were due to arrive from Aberdeen the following afternoon at Heathrow. The team were making their way out of the office to continue with house-to-house enquiries. He found a quiet corner and dialled the number. The phone was answered by Jack and Alan introduced himself. Jack sounded calm, he had a strong, softly spoken Scottish accent. Yes, he would see Alan at Heathrow. Yes, Margaret would accompany him although at the moment she was still very upset, only just having received the news from the local bobby. Alan tried to think of suitable words but could only manage, "I will arrange transport and accommodation, I will meet you at Heathrow tomorrow."

There was the sound of another voice in the background. Jack said, "It's the police in London, it's okay." There was a moment's silence, then more background speaking. Jack's voice came back on the line, it was clear and calm. "Thank you, we will see you tomorrow."

Alan slowly replaced the receiver. Before his mind could be flooded with the onrush of thoughts he flipped open the telephone directory and booked a room for two at the Clarendon Hotel, Blackheath to be charged to the MPS. It was usual in such circumstances to book much cheaper accommodation and there was a budget which was enforced, but you could lose your only child and grandchild just once in your life. No-one would question it.

Micky Banks was suddenly at Alan's shoulder. He turned to Alan.

"What's happening with the parents?"

"It's mum and step-dad. They are flying down from Aberdeen tomorrow." Micky replied, "I want you to meet them at the airport and arrange accommodation for them. The day after tomorrow they will identify the body."

"All done Guvnor. They are booked in to a hotel in Blackheath." The task of "family liaison" had not at this time been fully developed as a skill. No training was given and it was generally seen as a lumber.

Location of the murders of Samatha and Jazmine in Heathfield Terrace.

CHAPTER 4

The Case Settles

It was 2 am before Alan finally got to bed. His wife had long ago been immunised against odd working hours and sudden changes in routine. When he eventually did get back to his house, he could not resist going into each of his two boys' bedrooms, aged 12 and eight they slept peacefully, his younger son Robert on his back, face in the relaxed pose of innocence only a child possesses. Alan thought of Jazmine, a vision of blue lips and no breath presented itself. He needed sleep.

At 7 am Alan was back at Thamesmead, the office becoming familiar. A kettle, teapot and a motley collection of ropey looking cups had been conjured-up. Bob Thomas and the indexers were already hard at work, the carousel wheel now filling up, but still far short of being full. Alan made sure he had an unmarked police pool car available for the drive to Heathrow, his old Fiesta was totally unsuitable. He then joined John Bull who was about to give a briefing on the progress of the house-to-house enquiries.

In the meantime the actions began to be allocated. For every decision made, for every message received, for every statement written, an action was raised to qualify any anomaly or any further enquiry. These were handwritten and upon completion were handed back into the control room where they were analysed and either filed or made the subject of further action. Alan looked at the tray marked "DC Jackaman" and pulled out a sheaf of actions: top of the pile was to liaise with Samantha's parents.

He leafed through the actions, prioritising them. Some referred to visits to local known sex-offenders, others to the tracing of the yellow van. A picture of the van had now been made using the witness' description and old records of the type of GPO van used. A copy was circulated to all officers on the case. No such van had been seen again in or near Heathfield Terrace. It was not uncommon for vehicles to park in the cul-de-sac overnight and for drivers to sleep over.

In the late-afternoon Alan arrived at Heathrow Airport. He had contacted Special Branch and they had arranged for him to go airside to meet the Morrisons. It had started to rain, a thin drizzle which added to the sombre mood. The aircraft was on time and Alan stood at the foot of the aircraft's disembarkation steps. The Morrisons were the last to leave. Jack appeared first, wearing a dark blue suit, his long grey hair whipped up by a gust of wind, closely followed by Margaret who clung to the handrail, staring out as if unfocused. Jack took her arm and led her down the steps.

Alan introduced himself to Jack and shook hands. Margaret remained silent, Alan offered his hand and she took it, a soft, tired feel. Her eyes still unfocused. Alan walked with them both to the shelter of the terminal and awaited the arrival of their luggage. The time was filled with small talk between Jack and Alan, Margaret remained stalwartly quiet.

The journey back to the Clarendon Hotel, Blackheath was uneventful and an uncomfortable silence pervaded. Jack keeping Margaret company in the back of the car. It was early evening before Alan drove into the hotel car park which fronted Blackheath. Jack assisted Margaret whilst Alan heaved the suitcase from the boot and then led the way up the steps into the hotel foyer. The room key was handed over and Alan carried the case up followed by Jack. As they reached the room, Margaret started to wail, a deep keening, continuous, heart-rending wail. Alan opened the door and Jack put his arm around Margaret. She fought him off, slapping at his shoulders. Jack remained calm.

He turned to Alan, "I'm sorry. She's very upset and a couple of whiskeys on the plane which she's not used to."

Alan manoeuvred the suitcase inside the room. He said, "Please don't apologise. I will stay as long as you like, here is my number call me any time, night or day." He handed Jack his MPS murder team card. Jack looked-up, pain etched in his face, "Aye, we'll be okay, best if she has some rest." Alan shook Jack's hand. It seemed the only tiny crumb of comfort to offer. "I'll be back in the morning, 10 am."

"Aye, goodnight." Jack quietly closed the door, Alan could still faintly hear Margaret's low-pitched wail. It followed him down the corridor, it follows him still.

He was at Greenwich mortuary early the next morning. Before picking up Jack and Margaret he wanted to see what arrangements had been made to allow the viewing of the bodies. He was met by one of the coroner's officers and shown through to the chapel of rest. The chapel had a very church like ambience and was suitably hushed. Samantha's coffin was immediately visible. The door closed behind them and Alan took in the scene. Jazmine's coffin was a little distant from Samantha's, raised onto a dais. There were flowers placed by both coffins.

"Why are they not together?" Alan whispered.

The attendant, hands clasped together, whispered back, "We don't know how the parents will react. One is bad enough but seeing them together may prove too much."

Alan nodded and walked over to Samantha's coffin, the horror of the scene at Heathfield Terrace still vivid in his mind. To his relief the body of Samantha was wrapped in a white sheet, half of her head, the half with the most severe injuries was also covered in white sheeting concealing her most gruesome injuries but still exposing a blackened eye and a vicious cut near her chin.

Alan whispered, "Thanks for doing this, someone has gone to a great deal of effort." He remembered on previous cases where identification had been on a mortician's slab.

The attendant, obviously affected, spoke up a little. "The least we could do, especially considering the child." He nodded in the direction of the tiny coffin.

Alan walked over, he regretted wearing his leather soled shoes as they resounded on the flagged floor. One look. At rest. Blue lips. Followed by the coroner's assistant he left the room and once past the door to the chapel felt able to speak again at normal volume. He said, "I'm going to fetch the parents now, I'll be about and hour."

The assistant looking a little more relaxed since leaving the chapel replied, "We will be ready for you."

Alan drove the short distance across Blackheath to the Carlton Hotel and parked outside the main door. He went into reception and asked that a message be sent up to the room of Mr and Mrs Morrison that he was there. After only two minutes Jack came down, dressed in a navy blue suit, they shook hands. He looked a little flustered. "Can you give me a few minutes, Margaret isn't well. I'll go back up for her."

After an offer of help, which was declined, Jack went back up the stairs. Ten minutes later both he and Margaret came down, they were arguing, or at least Margaret was haranguing Jack.

Jack said, "She will be okay. I am afraid she has had a drink and she isn't supposed to."

Alan thought, "Who in God's heaven could blame her."

Margaret lurched from despair to moments of almost hysteria, at times seeming almost cheerful, this struck a discordant note. Alan sat them down in a quiet corner of the foyer and explained how he would drive them to Greenwich where they would meet the SIO Micky Banks. He would then take them to the mortuary to identify the bodies of Samantha and Jazmine. Alan, remembering the sight of Samantha's damaged face, decided not to steel them against what they were about to see, not just yet.

Alan took Margaret gently by the arm and led her down the hotel steps to the car where she got into the back with Jack. The drive back to the mortuary was quiet, punctuated by intermittent emotional outbursts by Margaret who was constantly being calmed by Jack. Alan parked the car on the double yellow lines and took the couple inside where Micky Banks was waiting in an ante room. Alan introduced them and left briefly to find the coroner's assistant. When he returned, they were deep in conversation with Banks who looked relieved to hand the grieving parents back to Alan.

Alan again briefly described what would happen, they would view the body of Margaret's daughter Samantha and she would be asked to formally identify her. They could be as long as they liked and leave whenever they liked. The instructions seemed surreal to Alan but Margaret and Jack nodded without saying anything. He then informed them that Samantha's body was mostly covered in a sheet to hide some of her injuries. Margaret and Jack looked stolidly forward without seeming to comprehend.

The coroner's assistant led the way to the chapel and opened the door. Alan went through followed by Jack holding Margaret's hand. Gritting his teeth, Alan walked over to where Samantha lay. Margaret and Jack stood by the coffin staring down. There were no tears. They stood silently for several minutes.

Alan forced himself to ask the question. "Margaret, is this Samantha?"

She stared down at the stony, waxen face of her dead daughter. Margaret visibly shuddered, she let out a deep sigh, nodded slowly and said, "Yes". She stayed a few moments longer and then turned to face the coffin of Jazmine. She walked slowly over to the tiny coffin and peered in. Her hand came up to her mouth and then fell away as she said, "Poor baby," and grasped Jack's hand.

"I think we'll go now Jack."

Out of the door, no dwelling any longer, back to the car and Alan drove them in complete silence to their hotel. As they walked back in Alan said to Jack, "I will pick you up at one and take you to the airport, in the meantime, is there anything I can do?"

Jack shook his head. "No. Thank you."

Alan watched as the couple made their way slowly, oh so slowly, up the hotel stairs.

The journey to Heathrow Airport was a sorrowful affair. Alan made sure they boarded their flight to Aberdeen and he then returned to the incident room at Thamesmead. He should have taken a formal statement of identification; he just didn't have the heart. It could be done at a later date. Meanwhile, he would write a statement to satisfy the enquiry for the time being.

A glance at the carousel showed more index cards, more sections. There was no need to ask for any update, the steady buzz of the incident room, a working beehive, nothing yet to mobilise it into ferocious activity. Alan picked up another half dozen or so actions, leafed through them, they all referred to eliminating known sex-offenders of which a trawl had been made of all those living locally. Already signs of desperation he thought, as he picked through the sad list.

The murder had been reported in the local newspaper, the *News Shopper*. It was front page and contained details of the yellow van. Already calls were coming in regarding possible sightings. At the early stage of any enquiry office meetings are regularly held and today was no different. Micky Banks updated the team, there were no direct suspects, Cosy had been all but eliminated ("Never say never"). It was now a waiting game, all was on hold pending the results from the scene, fingerprints and other forensics and hopefully results from the *post mortem* giving DNA.

The laboratory sergeant, Detective Sergeant Lionel Barclay who had been in charge of the scene at Heathfield Terrace voiced his concerns to Micky Banks of how there were some similarities to the murder on Wimbledon Common of Rachel Nickell in July of 1992.

Micky Banks arranged a meeting in the Wimbledon incident room on the 10th November 1993 with Detective Inspector Keith Pedder who was working on the Rachel Nickell murder. DI Pedder informed Banks they already had a suspect, Colin Stagg who lived locally to the murder scene at Wimbledon Common. However Pedder did take the opportunity to mention a criminal psychologist, Paul Britton, who had assisted them in developing a psychological profile for their suspect. Consequently a date was arranged for Britton to attend Thamesmead to discuss the Bisset case.

Paul Britton made the journey down from Leicester, it wasn't an auspicious start. He became hopelessly lost in the sprawl of Thamesmead amongst the high rise flats. When he eventually found the police station he was shocked at the sight of it. He later described it as being like a Portakabin extension on the "High School from Hell", thrown together and surrounded by a chain link fence. He parked his car in the safety of the compound and found Micky Banks wreathed in cigarette smoke ensconced in his minute office with the cardboard sign hanging askew on the door saying "SIO". An unnecessary affectation as everyone on the tightly knit squad knew whose lair it was.

Britton immediately sensed Banks reticence, deducing correctly that the calm, quiet, lined, tough-looking man before him was not a fan of psychological profiling. However, the niceties were met and Banks made Paul a cup of tea, which he poured into a suspicious looking, cracked and tannin stained mug. The rest of the team busied themselves in the next room, the ring of telephones and the drone of conversation a constant background hum. There was the occasional peal of laughter rising from the Stygian gloom of the main office to lighten the atmosphere. What anyone had to laugh about in a place like this was a mystery to Paul Britton.

Banks went through the circumstances of the case and showed the scene photographs. Until he saw the photographs, Britton had not realised how shocking the murders had been. The gruesome pictures opened his eyes to the reality. He saw this was no ordinary case as he studied the dreadful pictures of Samantha.

Banks puffed away on his roll-up as he pointed out a partial bloody shoeprint in the kitchen. He then turned to a shot of the bedroom. Paul Britton took a few moments before he realised that the tousled red hair peeking out of the duvet was that of a child laying on her front, head turned to the wall. Banks went on. "She was stripped, sexually-assaulted, re-dressed, put back to bed and then smothered, she is four-years-old." Using the present tense somehow added pathos. The two men stared at the photograph.

Paul Britton was stunned, he tried to gather his thoughts and apply his psychological training. He had seen nothing like it before. The only comparison which sprang to his mind was that of the final victim of Jack the Ripper and the now famous photograph of Mary Jane Kelly.

Banks gave Britton a full update as to where the enquiry now stood. Samantha's boyfriend Cosy, the unidentified old yellow van seen outside her flat, neighbours hearing the raised voices of a male and female coming from her flat at around 10.30 pm, a neighbour opposite hearing a scream at 3 am and seeing lights on in the flat. Samantha having disturbed an unknown man a fortnight earlier whom she caught looking into her flat as she was ironing. Banks continued, a pained expression on his lined face, "But, above all, now, over a week into the enquiry and we don't have a clue."

Banks then drove Paul Britton to the scene. After unlocking the police steel security door the two entered. Britton slowly walked from room-to-room making notes. Eerily quiet and cold, all the blood marks were still on the walls and floor. Jazmine's clothing still hung about, left to dry by caring hands, never to be worn. The cot stood forlornly in the bedroom. A child's crayon pictures clung to walls, held by Blu Tack. He noted that the rattan blind was rolled down over the living-room French window. This window gave access to a small balcony.

Britton broke the silence. "How do you think he got in?"

Micky Banks nodded in the direction of the front door. "I think he probably conned his way in the front door. Either that or it was someone she knew. There is no sign of a forced entry and he attacked her in the hall." The large pooling of blood next to the front door which still stained the carpet made this first analysis the most likely.

The two men left the gloomy flat and returned to Thamesmead under an appropriately dark, overcast sky. They went to the tiny office where Banks took up his seat behind his document laden desk. He had put a dossier of copies of statements and *post mortem* photographs together for Paul Britton to take away with him. Banks was fairly sure Samantha knew her killer. He explained how a neighbour had reported to Social Services how she was having visits from different men at odd hours.

Banks lit another cigarette. "She may have been on the game, not big time. Just starting out, on the fringes." He rifled through some of the documents on his desk. "We have found letters and newspaper adverts." He shoved one such over the desk to Britton. It was a photocopy of an advert in the *Greenwich and Eltham Mercury*:

> "Single mother, 27, needs friends. I'm an honest reliable, artistic ex hippy who smokes roll ups and doesn't eat meat."

Banks scowled over the desk. "That was in early 93, They progressed to this." He pushed another sheet across the desk. It was an advert in the *London Weekly Advertiser* dated 8–14th September.

> "Up market, tall, erotic blonde escort, 27, and aching to hear from you generous men. Just tell me what you want. All letters answered."

"And this." Another sheet crossed the desk.

"Young sexy long legged blonde requires a nice gentleman with spare cash to pay small child's Scholl [sic] fees in return for regular, discreet, no strings, fun liaisons. Cannot accommodate. Very Genuine."

Banks looked up at Britton. "Now I am not saying she was on the game, but these don't make it look good. The press already have had a sniff and are backing away. Just when we need their help."

Paul Britton gathered the documents and made his way through to the car park. Once he had counted the wheels on his car he drove off back to Leicester to consider what he had just been made privy to.

The net was spreading wider, all Samantha's known associates, both from now and deep into her past. Any known lovers, disputes, neighbours who had a grudge. It was clear that this was not going to be an easy enquiry, once the net started to spread it was apparent the investigation was struggling.

Alan thought back to the murder scene. Again the thought pecking away, this is no "domestic", this is something unfathomable, beyond anything he had ever investigated.

The next line of enquiry, who was Samantha Bisset?

POLICE APPEAL FOR ASSISTANCE

MURDER

On the morning of Thursday 4 November 1993 the bodies of Samantha Bisset (27) and her daughter, Jazmine (4) were found at their home at 1A Heathfield Terrace, Plumstead, SE18. They had been brutally murdered.

Samantha and Jazmine were last seen alive at about 3.40pm on Wednesday 3 November. Did you see them alive later that evening?

DID YOU KNOW
SAMANTHA BISSET?
DO YOU KNOW WHO
COULD HAVE KILLED HER
AND 4 YEAR OLD JAZMINE?
CAN YOU HELP?

Please contact the Incident Room at

THAMESMEAD POLICE STATION
TEL: 081•312 1200

OR RING

CRIMESTOPPERS 0800 555 111

METROPOLITAN POLICE

Police appeal poster in the murder of Samantha and Jazmine Bisset.

CHAPTER 5

Who was Samantha?

The only child of Margaret and Douglas Bisset, Samantha was born in Dundee on 25th February 1967. From an early age she showed leanings towards an artistic nature. In this she followed her father who had been a successful freelance artist specialising in watercolours. She had a comfortable childhood and showed academic promise.

The idyll came to an abrupt end when her father died suddenly in 1980 when Samantha was at the impressionable age of 14. She moved with her Scottish mother to Margaret's home town of Dundee. Samantha found the move disruptive, she didn't settle into her new school. Her poor academic results started to reflect her unhappiness and she left secondary school without any qualifications. Her relationship with her mother became strained and she spent most of her time and her happiest moments with her grandmother. Meanwhile Margaret met Jack Morrison and remarried in 1985. Jack welcomed Samantha into their new home, and the arrangement did go some way to steadying Samantha, although she never again studied diligently. In her late teens she started to mix with youngsters who were into the drug scene in Dundee.

With the added complication of drugs Samantha became ever less manageable at home. At the earliest opportunity she left school, home and Scotland and went to the south of England where she joined what was then a thriving community of hippies who travelled the country in old busses visiting various open air music festivals and generally living a hand-to-mouth existence. Her exact movements over this period were vague, even to Samantha.

She would still visit Margaret and Jack on occasion in Dundee. Her appearances were generally out of the blue. As time progressed they became ever more sporadic and her lifestyle was slipping into the taking of more and heavier drugs. Jack and Margaret would remonstrate with her and try to encourage her to stay in Dundee, but Samantha had developed into a headstrong young woman and would always drift off back to her hippy world.

She stayed with various groups around the south coast of England and for a while lived in a community in central Wales which had established itself in a semi-permanent way by purchasing land and living a Bohemian existence in wigwams. There were several of these alternative communities springing up at the time and Samantha travelled freely between them. By 1986, aged 19, the attractions of the hippy lifestyle were wearing thin and Samantha decided to break away. She succeeded in obtaining a job in an old people's home in Salisbury. Whilst working there she met Anne Hesketh who was to become a lifelong friend. Mrs Hesketh lived nearby with her husband and children. After a while Samantha moved in with them, paying her way by acting as a nanny to the children.

By June 1987 Samantha was feeling restless and decided to give the hippy lifestyle another try. The summer was blossoming and the pull of the free wheeling life was calling her again. She was young enough to only think of the positives and never the down side. Against Anne's wishes she moved out and took up with one of the many travelling troops around Salisbury. These bands swelled in the summer and shrunk as the bad weather approached. They attracted an eclectic mix of devotees. Some committed to the change of society, others more interested in selling drugs and taking advantage of vulnerable, naïve aesthetes, such as Samantha.

During her travelling Samantha met another like-minded soul Russell Beattie. The relationship waxed and waned with the summer. As autumn approached Samantha gravitated back to her friend Anne Hesketh where she was welcomed. Unfortunately for Samantha, she had become ever more drug dependent and by the spring of 1988 her drug dependency had become acute. Mrs Hesketh worried for Samantha but could not support her with a drug problem. She had small children and was worried for their safety. She persuaded Samantha to attend drug counselling.

Samantha took her advice and went on a rehabilitation course in Southampton. It was whilst in Southampton she met social worker Andrew McNeil. The two made a decision to live together and moved to London where they took up residence in a room at 497 Woolwich Road, south east London. Samantha again started to rely more and more upon drugs, the relationship between her and McNeil did not last and he returned to his family home in Hampshire.

After McNeil had left, Samantha found herself to be pregnant. The news of this was not enough to tempt McNeil back to her side. He did not feel he was able to support Samantha financially and, Samantha, showing her typically stubborn streak, would not pursue the matter. It was at this stage that her strong willpower really came into effect. She took stock of her situation. She was without support, drug dependant and expecting a child. This setback had a life transforming effect on the 22-year-old Samantha.

A lesser person would have simply collapsed under such odds, but not Samantha, she immediately foreswore drugs and progressed to kick the habit. She moved into a hostel for single mothers at Adair House, Shooters Hill, Woolwich and she met Conrad Ellam known to everyone as Cosy who, despite her circumstances, became her steady boyfriend.

Jazmine was born on 20th July 1989 without complications at Green-wich District hospital. Not letting up, Samantha managed to persuade the authorities to give her a flat. This was at 1a, Heathfield Terrace, Plum-stead, and she moved in with Jazmine on 21st August 1989. She promised to herself and to Jazmine that she would devote her life to the upbring-ing and welfare of her daughter. The child was adored.

A steadier relationship developed between herself and her mother with a pattern of regular telephone calls on Sundays. Margaret and Jack came to visit her and Jazmine in Plumstead. Jack offered financial help and the offer was open for Samantha to return to Scotland. Samantha made it clear she wanted to stay where she was and proceeded to turn her flat into a comfortable, safe home for Jazmine.

Samantha would save money to visit her parents in Scotland and all who met Jazmine wondered at the health and happiness of her and her mother. Samantha never ever reverted to taking drugs. As Samantha became more settled she started to think how she could provide for a better life for Jazmine. She started to research private education. She also attended photographic model studios with the aim of earning money modelling. Although good looking and tall, this was perhaps a fantasy. Other money making schemes were then tried. She advertised in local magazines and newspapers as what can only be described as an escort. She told friends she was looking for a "Sugar Daddy". Someone to provide Jazmine with the start in life she needed.

Cosy Ellam was a true friend, but they never became a real couple; although Cosy was very kind and good to Jazmine, he was not what Samantha was looking for. She sought financial security of the kind Cosy, hard working and devoted as he was, could not provide. Jazmine was entered into a local nursery and Samantha and Cosy would share the child care. Sometimes Cosy would stay over at the flat but as often as not would go home to his parents' house, but was always available and happy to help Samantha.

There was little doubt that Samantha wasn't being entirely honest with Cosy. She was undoubtedly very fond of him and he in turn was helpful and kind to both her and her daughter. But, since Jazmine's birth, she had developed an over-riding ambition to make a better life for Jazmine. She had started to advertise in newspaper "lonely hearts" columns. Some of these adverts were found in papers recovered from her flat. The adverts were circled in ink. Some were quite innocent, as an example in the *Greenwich and Eltham Mercury*:

> "Single mother, 27, needs friends. I'm an honest, reliable ex-hippy who smokes roll ups and doesn't eat meat."

They became more explicit, as in the *London Weekly Advertiser*:

> "Up-market, tall, erotic blonde escort, and aching to hear from you generous men. Just tell me what you want. All letters answered."

This was dated 8–14 September only six weeks before her murder. Another advert in a contact magazine read:

"Young sexy, long legged blonde requires a nice gentleman with spare cash to pay small child's school fees in return for regular, discreet, no strings, fun liaisons. Cannot accommodate. Very genuine."

This referred to her application for Jazmine to attend a private school in Sussex where she hoped to work as a helper to assist with fees. The underlying reason for everything in her life at this time was Jazmine.

Samantha was due in a few weeks to go on holiday with Cosy and Jazmine to the Gambia. Her mother Margaret had forwarded her £1,000 to pay for the trip. Samantha had overcome her reservations of accepting money from her mother as she saw it of benefit to Jazmine. Both she and Cosy were excited with the prospect and greatly looking forward to the trip.

Jazmine and Samantha Bisset.

CHAPTER 6

The Day of the Murders

Wednesday 3rd November was windy with occasional showers, a dull mundane autumn day which Samantha had to herself. She had taken Jazmine in the morning to Abbey Wood Nursery; an expense which she was determined to afford as Jazmine was thriving there. She looked out of the balcony windows which faced onto the rear of the block. Being at ground level the light was limited. The rattan blind over the balcony window was firmly set in the rolled-up position. It had ceased to function properly weeks before and Cosy had secured it in the up position, using the defunct pull string. She gazed out at the patch of grass which led down to a line of trees. Whilst the light lasted she would save on electricity. Meat Loaf was playing on the radio, *I'd Do Anything for Love.* She swayed her way to a pile of precariously balanced books next to an old sofa. They were mostly on self-sufficiency and herb growing, she idly picked one up, *The Benefits of Vinegar in the Modern World.*

The old days of the hippy commune still held an attraction for her, she romanticised the idea of the New Age life but she had spent enough time involved in it to remember the bad aspects. The drug dependency, she mostly remembered the awful weather, life really wasn't so bad in her little flat, complete with Jazmine. She replaced the book and picked-up from the top of the pile a pamphlet about holidays in the Gambia. She had been discussing with Cosy the previous evening the forthcoming holiday there. The idea appealed to her travelling spirit and it would be a tremendous experience for Jazmine. Looking out of the window she visualised sunny beaches.

Spinning around, within five paces she was in the kitchen. She checked the clock, never having bothered with a watch. It was five minutes to three, two minutes before she had to go and pick up Jazmine. The Meat Loaf track was coming to an end, she smiled to herself. Another rocker who had sold out to the industry, so unlike her New Age friends and memories of free and easy music sessions on long summer evenings in the New Forest. Her gaze swept to a writing pad appended to a small white notice board. She picked out a business card tucked into the top of the pad. ABC Cabs. The telephone was attached to the wall next to the pad and she punched the number into the phone's keypad.

A gruff south London voice ground out the name, "ABC Cabs."

She asked for a cab to pick her up from Abbey Wood Nursery at 3.30 pm. This was a small indulgence she allowed herself. The voice at the other end mechanically repeated the order and asked for a name. Replacing the telephone she checked her purse, she knew the fare was going to be £3, and she had enough. Turning off the radio and snatching her coat from a peg behind the front door she donned it, then, after a moment's hesitation, took down two brightly coloured scarves and wrapped them around her neck. She patted her coat pocket ensuring she had her key and stepped out into the gloomy day. She pulled the door shut behind her, hearing the click as the lock engaged.

The walk to Abbey Wood took 25 minutes; she swept along with an easy grace, a tall slim woman who was naturally attractive without making any obvious attempts to be so. It was not raining but the threat was there, the onset of evening already detectable in the overcast sky. Her clothing, another remnant of her New Age years, a long dark coat over a flower-patterned raffia skirt, brightly-coloured stockings and scarves. She wore no headwear over her long straight blond hair. Her gait was that of a country girl, an easy confident swing, head held up as if waltzing down a traffic free country lane. She encountered no-one she knew on her way to the gates of Abbey Wood Nursery, where, upon arrival, she was as usual one of the first mothers to arrive. She had never mixed socially with any of the other women but nodded to one or two in recognition.

The doors of the nursery opened and out ran a gaggle children, Samantha only had eyes for one. The ever smiling Jazmine, almost chubby, a mop of unkempt dark blond hair tied back in a pony tail, never doubting her mother would be there to greet her she ran over, eager to relate what had happened in the last two hours. In her hand she clasped a picture, laboriously drawn in crayon. She held it up for approval.

"Lovely, darling"

Another one to add to the growing gallery of Jazmine's works of art adorning the walls of their flat. Samantha crouched down and wrapped one of her scarves around Jazmine's neck. She took the drawing and walked out to the road where the cab was just pulling up. She waved, ensuring nobody else grabbed it as the rain was starting to come down a little harder. She opened the rear door and Jazmine scrambled in. The cab driver turned his head, almost imperceptibly,

"Mrs Bisset?"

Not wishing to enter into a discussion on her marital status, Samantha replied, "Yes, Heathfield Terrace, please." She sat back ready to enjoy the ride. The cab accelerated away, a little too quickly thought Samantha and instinctively pulled Jazmine close to her. In less than ten minutes they pulled into the service road at Heathfield Terrace and stopped outside the flat. The cab driver looked at the car's clock, it was 3.40 pm. Samantha had the exact fare ready and handed it over to the outstretched hand of the driver. She helped Jazmine from the cab, shouted a thankyou and slammed the car door. The taxi did a three point turn and sped off to the next call. The cab driver was the last person to see Samantha and Jazmine before their murder.

Samantha ducked her head against the cold wind sweeping in from the common. No-one else was visible, she could feel her large looped earrings flapping against her face. With Jazmine in tow she walked quickly to the steps which led down to her flat. One hand gripped the rail, the other Jazmine's hand. Once safely at the door she felt in her pocket for the key and opened it. She switched on the hall light and unwrapped Jazmine who bolted down toward the living-room where she could watch her favourite children's TV with Andy Peters. Samantha hung their coats on the hallway peg and followed Jazmine into the living-room where she turned on the TV, then the gas fire.

There were no letters on the mat. Still no hoped for reply from her application for entry to the private school in Sussex. Her hopes were still high she could obtain a job within the school where Jazmine would board, thus reducing the fees. Cosy hadn't been very hopeful of its success and did not see himself moving to Sussex.

There were other things in Samantha's life of which Cosy was unaware. Apart from the advertising in newspaper lonely heart columns she had been out with a couple of men who had replied to the advertisements. They had been pleasant enough, but did not fit the expectation Samantha had in mind, someone who would fulfil her ambitions for Jazmine.

One of the hopefuls was expected to call her this evening, Samantha had decided he would not be able to provide enough for her dreamed expectations and had decided to end it before it went any further. Ever the optimist she was hoping for further replies from others. She smiled to herself, "Fish to fry." She was Pisces after all.

Cosy was also unaware of the visit to the professional photographer who had taken her "glamour" photographs two months previously. She had had to scrimp to afford them in the London studio. Despite the gushing optimism of the photographer their circulation hadn't resulted in a single reply. She went to the drawer in the living-room where they were kept and opened the photo album. They were indeed rather good, decorous under soft lighting, fully-clothed. She replaced the folder and went back to the kitchen where she made a cup of tea and beans on toast.

Joining Jazmine on the sofa they both watched TV whilst eating their toast. Jazmine then picked a spot on the wall to hang her latest work of art. There would soon be insufficient space for them all and the time would come when Samantha would have to secretly start removing them. She baulked at the idea.

The evening wore on and the rain eased. The darkness outside became all enveloping. The useless blind stayed in the up position and there were no other curtains, giving perfect vision into the living-room to any person foolhardy enough to stand in the open grass area behind the flat. Cosy had tried unsuccessfully to fix the blinds. Samantha told him not to worry about it, nobody would go to the effort of going round the back to stare in, and even if they did there was nothing to see. Samantha had never been security-minded and believed fervently in the innate good in people. The balcony doors were hardly ever secured and the front door was never double locked.

Jazmine was always tired after a day at the nursery. Samantha prepared her for bed and after bath time dressed her in her old long sleeved red top and yellow panties. They settled down again in front of the TV. John Major was telling the nation that after years of troubles there was an end in sight to the terrorism in Northern Ireland. Samantha turned the TV off and read to Jazmine, the current book was *Swallows and Amazons*. She was so proud of the progress Jazmine was making with her reading, already learning letters and recognising words. At 7 pm she took her to her room. There were only two bedrooms and Jazmine had a cot in one with a made up bed next to it which she and Samantha shared until she fell asleep. Samantha gently placed her in her cot and leaving the door ajar went back to the living-room.

There were no telephone callers that night. No knights to the rescue. Cosy was at work in the dye factory and she expected him to drop by in the morning. Samantha prepared herself for bed. Dressed in her night dress she sat in the living-room. She thought of her forthcoming holiday in the Gambia. She felt a pang of guilt about Cosy, he was a good man and was very good with Jazmine. The blackness of the window reflected only her own reflection giving the false impression that, as she could not see out, no-one could see in.

The silent phone hung defiantly on wall. At 8.47 pm Samantha lifted the receiver and made the comfort call she often made, to her star sign. There were still aspects of New Age mysticism she was loath to abandon. The recorded message clicked in:

"Pisces; The future although uncertain at present will soon be made clear. A new acquaintance you will meet will have a life changing influence on your plans."

She smiled. Not bad. Reassured she looked in at Jazmine who was sleeping peacefully. Samantha prepared herself for bed, sleeping next to her.

A neighbour heard the sound of washing-up clattering in Samantha's kitchen sink at 11 pm. At about 3 am a neighbour who resided in Revell Rise which backed onto the green at the rear of Samantha's flat was woken by screams and what she described as a commotion. Looking out of her window she saw the lights on at 1a Heathfield Terrace. As soon as it started, the screaming stopped. The witness went back to bed.

CHAPTER 7

The Day After the Day After

The results of the first *post mortem* were starting to filter in. Unsurprisingly death had been caused by multiple stab wounds. Two weapons were used, both thinly bladed, one with a width of 1 centimetre, the other 2.5. Both weapons would have been ten centimetres in length. It was possible that those inflicted after the victim's death had been caused by a larger third weapon. No weapon of such description had been found at the scene. All kitchen knives from the flat had been submitted to the forensic laboratory and none of them showed any evidence of being used in the crime, they were of a cheap and flimsy make, totally unsuited for the heavy cuts inflicted.

Roger Boydell-Smith and Lionel Barclay had been present at the first *post mortem* and noted the peculiar angle of the body after reconstruction. They voiced the opinion that a piece of it was missing. As a result a second *post mortem* was undertaken by Dr Hill on 10th November. Dr Hill was unable to positively say a part of the body was missing.

Micky Banks was still of the opinion a section of flesh was missing and requested a third *post mortem* which was carried out by Dr Dick Shepherd on 10th November. Samantha's body was deconstructed and re-assembled. Dr Shepherd found conclusively, as the investigating officers had suspected, that an area from her abdominal wall was missing. Dr Shepherd estimated it measured 10 cm x 12 cm. The news of the missing piece of flesh was greeted with alarm by the team and further reinforced the suspicion that the perpetrator had taken a trophy of his unspeakable deed. It was decided to keep this information within the walls of the enquiry team. Dr Shepherd's other findings supported Dr Hill. In

Shepherd's opinion there were a number of features of the injuries which clearly indicated this was a sexually-motivated attack.

Of prime importance was the indication of after death mutilation, in particular, of her thighs breasts and genitalia. Removal of a portion of skin (as a trophy) and the "blitz"-style of stabbing suggested that the attack was sexually-motivated.

The crime scene forensic report was also made available, written by Dr Kamala De Soyza. Her conclusions were that Samantha had been killed whilst standing outside the kitchen door in the hallway; indicated by the heavy pooling of blood. There had been a second attack at a low level indicated by blood splatters on the cupboard opposite the bedroom. She had been dragged into the living-room. Diluted blood was found in both the kitchen and bathroom sinks indicating the perpetrator had washed in both. The only DNA results from seminal stains matched Cosy Ellam. Jazmine's vaginal swabs were stained with blood indicating she had been sexually-assaulted prior to being suffocated.

The house-to-house enquiries had failed to find anyone who had seen who it was who had entered the flat. The only snippet of information to go on was the presence of the mysterious yellow ex-GPO van. It was certainly a pointer as it had a link to Samantha's hippy past but with no index or even a partial index number it was going to be struggle to identify it.

Publicity was the key and local newspapers carried an artists impression of the van complete with home made side windows. The murder achieved front page news in the weekly *News Shopper*, after that the press showed little interest, even at a local level.

After the second day of the investigation, Micky Banks called for a briefing. The team gathered in the gloomy room at Thamesmead where he updated everyone on the latest information coming in. There then followed the usual "round robin" of all those present. There was still no news on the identity of the yellow van, as each officer took their turn it was a case of elimination but no new leads. The conclusion was that the attack had been pre-planned and pre-meditated utilising some surveillance. It was highly probable the attacker was unknown to the victim. The enquiry team had on its books a classic, psychopathic killer. A highly dangerous individual who without doubt would strike again. They didn't have any idea who it was.

CHAPTER 8

No Suspect in the Frame

And so the enquiry moved on. A week had passed and no credible suspect was found who the team could focus their efforts upon. Instead, the actions were churned out along the lines of visiting all known associates of Samantha, tracking those who had answered any of her adverts in the lonely hearts columns. The lead on the yellow GPO van was taking shape. All such vans which had been sold into auctions were traced on the national database to see whether any were registered in the area of south east London.

Press interest quickly fell away completely even at a local level. There were no reports in the national press or on regional TV. After the one front page spread in the local *News Shopper* no further enquiries were made by local journalists into the case. Even the MPS itself seemed to take little interest above the local level. It is usual for murder enquiries to be allocated an operation name. The Bisset enquiry never was and became just that, "The Bisset Enquiry".

An assumption had been made that Samantha was a woman of easy virtue and in some quarters it was even put about she was involved in prostitution. The fact that she was a single mother who had been a drug addict, living in a council flat in an unfashionable part of London, did nothing to whet the appetite of any news hound. In fairness it wasn't public knowledge just how extreme and unusual the attack had been.

Lack of press coverage is a two-edged sword. The press can be intrusive and slow the investigation, even to the extent of developing their own, sometimes half-baked theories, and, just as quickly veering off in another direction; the plus side being that with press interest the case is given oxygen. This can result in positive information coming into the incident room and so long as there is public interest the case will continue to be investigated.

The scene had now been fully forensicated, including fingerprinting, these were checked against the National Criminal Index. The majority of the fingerprints were those of small children. Visitors to the flat since Samantha and Jazmine moved in were painstakingly identified and detectives were despatched to interview them all and take elimination fingerprints. Incredibly, every fingerprint lifted in the flat was identified, including those of all the children. This is almost unheard of, there are usually always fingerprints from crime scenes that just never get identified.

Only one person of real interest was identified, Peter Copley was a man who had known Samantha for only a short time and had become friendly with her, he had visited her at her flat and had also met her on other occasions. Alan was sent to interview him. On arrival at the house in Abbey Wood Alan was invited in by a stocky man in his thirties, he was well spoken. He admitted knowing and meeting Samantha and said he had a high regard for her. During the interview he appeared nervous and was initially reluctant to make a written statement but did so eventually, in which he claimed on the night of the murder he was visiting his ex-wife in Sussex.

Upon his return to Thamesmead, Alan spoke to the office manager and as a result an action was raised to verify the man's alibi. Alan checked the timing of the man's drive to visit his family in Sussex. From the time he had left Abbey Wood he would have arrived at his destination at about 9 pm. Copley stated he was in bed by midnight. It was a close call but it would have been possible for him to have left Sussex in the early hours unseen and drive to Heathfield Terrace, commit the murders and drive back to Sussex before anyone there was aware of his absence. His alibi of arrival and his stay overnight was confirmed. Micky Banks called Alan into his office.

Alan stood before the desk. There was no chair. Banks puffed away at a cigarette, his face serious. Pressure was beginning to mount upon him for a result in the case. Banks had had a bad day in any event as one of the detectives on the team who was involved in a search of a property on Shooters Hill had been entrusted with an exhibit, a pair of women's panties. The detective had unaccountably lost them. Although it was unlikely that the exhibit had anything to do with the case, it was the sort of mistake which could mean the difference between closing a case or not. Micky was in the process of deciding the fate of the detective. He looked-up from the statement Alan had taken from Peter Copley.

"What do you think Al?"

"Well Guvnor, he seems straight up to me. He was definitely nervous but that is understandable, given the circumstances. Circumstance which he knew about by the way, he had heard from making his own enquiries about how she was cut up but didn't know the details. The alibi in Sussex bears up, but, it is just possible for him to have driven back here in the night, killed Samantha and returned to Sussex before light. However, he hardly knew Samantha and has no history of violence. Not even a temper. It's a big call for him to drive all the way from Sussex and then return without anyone knowing. It's a hell of a risky way to create an alibi." Banks sat back in his chair, he took another long drag of his cigarette and blew the smoke skyward. "Alright Al, go back and see this bloke again. Put a bit of pressure on him." The interview was over.

Alan went back to the incident room. The desk he shared was free and he grabbed it. He dialled the number of Peter Copley and waited. The phone was answered. "Hello Mr Copley, it's DC Jackaman here from the Samantha enquiry. Is it possible to see you again today?" There was a pause. "But I've just given you a statement, there's nothing else I can add."

Alan jumped in, "Just a couple of things we need to clear up."

Another pause, "Am I a suspect?"

Alan thought, "Everyone's a suspect" but replied "Oh no Mr Copley, Only something which I can't discuss on the phone. Would this afternoon be convenient?"

Another pause, "Well if it's necessary."

"Okay, see you at one o'clock."

Alan reflected, were those pauses cause for suspicion, is Peter Copley trying to hide something. At five minutes to one he drove up in his Fiesta to Copley's house. Copley answered the door before Alan could knock.

They went into the living-room where Copley started the conversation. "How can I help? She was a lovely person and I will do anything. Do you have any idea who may be responsible?"

Alan took out Copley's statement. "I need to go over a few of the times again." Peter Copley went into greater detail, he was going to see Samantha that day but had at the last minute decided against it. Yes the times he had given were absolutely correct. He had witnesses who saw him leave London and his ex-wife could verify his arrival in Sussex. Yes he had stayed overnight, had a good breakfast the following morning and had then spent the day taking-out his children down in Sussex. It wasn't until two days later he had heard of Samantha's murder.

Alan approached the story from different angles and tried to shake the account but the story remained the same. As Alan left Copley announced he was conducting his own enquiries locally and if he found out anything he would let the police know. Alan drove back toward Thamesmead, before turning into the road of the police station he stopped, turned off the engine and thought hard. He didn't believe Copley had anything to do with Samantha's death. Back in Micky Banks office he explained what he had found. Banks sat back. "Well I don't like it," he said.

"Guvnor, I have interviewed him twice. He just doesn't fit the bill. How could anyone sneak out of a house miles away, commit a murder and return unnoticed, covered in blood, then calmly sit down to breakfast and then take the kids out?" Banks looked annoyed. "He's the best we've got. But," he looked thoughtful, "it's not enough to bring him in. Keep an eye on him, and prompt him to come forward with any information." Alan was relieved he hadn't been asked to take the matter further.

The office meetings became ever more depressing. Every lead was researched and eliminated. The news from forensics was not much better. Because of the extent of injuries to Samantha it had been impossible to determine if there had been any sexual penetration. No sperm traces could be found and hence no possibility of DNA evidence. No other source of potential DNA evidence was forthcoming. Despite a microscopic examination, no foreign DNA was discovered on the body.

An officer had been sent to obtain a set of fingerprints from the body of Samantha. Never an easy task, known as a "dead set" it was made even more difficult by the peculiar leathery nature of her skin. This was caused by the massive blood loss. In any event the prints taken were not of sufficient quality for comparison in the fingerprint department. Roger Boydell-Smith then attempted to take them. By this time the skin of the hands had become so stiff it proved an impossible task. At the recommendation of Detective Sergeant Barclay an application was made to the coroner Sir Montague Levine to sever a hand in order to make the taking of the prints easier. This can be done by inflating the hand with water.

This was not long after the *Marchioness* tragedy where the victims had had their hands severed to aid identification but without the knowledge of their next of kin. The incident provoked a great deal of criticism of the insensitivity of the police. The appropriate permissions were obtained for Samantha and the application to sever the left hand was granted. By the time it was granted it was very late in the evening before the hand was taken from the body. It was placed in an exhibit bag but there was nowhere to store it before taking it to have fingerprints lifted.

Barclay suggested to Roger that he take it home and leave it in his fridge overnight. Roger at first thought Lionel was joking but there was really no other secure alternative. The hand rested, unknown to Mrs Boydell-Smith, in the family fridge overnight before Roger rose very early the next morning to take it to fingerprint branch. The end result was a set of prints which could be used to eliminate the victim's fingerprints from the scene.

One positive outcome of the scene search was the shoeprint, in blood, of an Adidas training shoe. It was only a partial print, a detailed search had revealed other fragments of the shoeprint around the flat. A composite printout was constructed of all the footprint fragments. It revealed the killer was wearing Adidas training shoes. The important aspect of this was that at least it ruled out half the population as the killer was probably male.

The house-to-house enquiries were coming to an end. The only information of significance was that screams were heard briefly at 3 am. Shortly afterwards another witness claimed to have heard the sound of two voices from the direction of Samantha's flat, both male, as if arguing. One was shouting, "Leave it, I said leave it."

An Adidas training shoeprint of the exact pattern found at the crime scene.
It was discovered on pages from the *Daily Mirror* TV supplement during re-investigation (*Chapter 11*) and matched the earlier
composite pieced together from fragments in blood (*Chapter 8*).

CHAPTER 9

What Have We Got?

On the discovery of a murder, in most cases a suspect is identified within 24 hours. If not, then once the machinery of the investigation gets under way the identity of the suspect will become clear in the first week. If this does not prove to be the case then the SIO knows they may be in trouble and has on his hands something known as a "sticker". That is to say the enquiry team have no positive leads as to who was responsible.

In the modern era all murder investigations are subject to review. These are instigated if, after 28 days from the time of the murder, or discovery of the body, no-one is charged. There was no review procedure in 1993 and the murders of Samantha and Jazmine Bisset had fallen into the sticker category.

Alan was called in to see Micky Banks. Micky puffed away on his roll-up cigarette and looked up as Alan entered. His face was expressionless as he pointed at the phone lying on his paper strewn desk.

"Someone from finance department at the Yard wants a word."

Alan picked up the receiver.

"DC Jackaman."

The voice at the other end spoke quickly with an angry edge.

"Are you the officer who authorised two people to stay at the Clarendon Hotel?"

Alan bridled at the word "people".

"I am."

"On whose authority?"

"My own."

"Well," the pompous voice continued, "You had no authority."

Alan looked across the desk at Banks who was reclining in his chair watching the proceedings impassively.

Alan continued, "They were important witnesses in a murder enquiry we are investigating."

The voice cut in. "As I understand it, they are not witnesses, merely the parents of the victim." Alan started to feel anger rise up. "They were required to identify the bodies. That makes them witnesses."

The voice riposted, "That doesn't make them *important* witnesses, only *important* witnesses can be housed at the police expense and only then with prior authority."

Alan watched Banks, who gave no clue as to which side of the fence he was on. "Who is this?" he asked, keeping his voice calm.

"Finance department," came the reply.

"No. Who is speaking?"

There was a moment's silence before the voice gave a name.

Alan continued, "I stand by my decision, the witnesses were an essential part of the enquiry. If there are any further questions address them in writing to my boss Detective Superintendent Banks."

Bank's eye-brows raised a fraction.

"Be assured I will." The voice was still speaking as Alan hung up the phone. He fixed Banks with a stare and said, "What a prick."

Banks burst into laughter. "Well done Al."

That day's office meeting required all to attend. The team was already thinning, those officers from crime squads who had assisted in the initial house-to-house enquiries had returned to their respective police stations. Bryan Reeve called the meeting to order. The general atmosphere was one of tiredness. Each officer was asked for updates as Bob Thomas kept minutes. At the end of the "round robin" Banks addressed the room: "We are two weeks into this enquiry now and a credible suspect has still to be identified. We all know the horrendous background to this case. The press hasn't shown any particular interest and although they may have their uses we will use their lack of interest to our advantage. All press liaison will be done through Bryan or myself, no-one else to talk to the press." There was a murmur of shared agreement.

Banks went on to describe what was known and the way the enquiry would move forward. Starting with Samantha, the enquiries would continue with the adverts in magazines and to search any other possible outlets she may have used. It was of paramount importance to identify and interview all those who had responded to her contact points in newspapers and magazines. A list of telephone numbers in and out of the flat at Heathfield Terrace going back over a year had been drawn up and the process of attaching names to corresponding telephone numbers was well under way with the intention of interviewing all those identified. Samantha's past history was being scrutinised, including the father of Jazmine, her New Age contacts who were spread around the country, her local friends and their associates.

Enquiries were to continue into the mysterious yellow van. A sketch had been drawn by a witness. This had been compared to all vans used by the GPO. From that list was defined the probable make and model. All of those were to be checked to see if they were still registered and the owners seen and eliminated. There were over 300 of them.

The composite shoeprint of an Adidas trainer was to be researched. Where was it made? How many were made? Where was it distributed and where were the outlets? The composite shoeprint was to be circulated to all Metropolitan Police stations to be checked against any burglar arrested wearing the same type of trainer. The size had been estimated as a 7. Unusually small for a male, but, it was also stressed this was not exact and could be as large as a 9. There were many variables which made being precise on shoe sizes difficult to determine. However the declaration of size 7 had been mentioned and some within the enquiry mistakenly fixed that as the actual size.

It was apparent from the information of the pathologist Dr Shepherd and the forensic examiner Dr De Soyza that the offender was predictably a sexual psychopath, therefore a list had been compiled of all local sex-offenders who would be seen and asked to alibi themselves. A further search was to made nationwide of all similar offences to find if any them were still outstanding and carried the same hallmarks.

Next on the agenda was the missing piece of flesh coupled with the theory that the offender must have carried out some form of surveillance on Samantha's flat prior to the murder. A thorough search of the surrounding common and woodland was required to find possible likely locations for viewing the victim's flat and any associated hideaway areas for the missing knives and flesh.

One further nugget from the crime scene examiner about where exactly within the flat Samantha had been initially attacked was cleared-up by close examination of Cosy's statement. Because of the massive pooling of blood just inside the front door it had been assumed that Samantha had somehow opened the door to allow her attacker access. This scenario initially reinforced the theory that the attacker was somebody who was known to her. Known well enough for her to open the door and allow whoever it was access to her flat. This assumption did not fit with the fact that the front door was double locked when Cosy arrived in the morning.

Closer examination of the scene demonstrated by blood splatter distribution showed that Samantha had been stabbed next to the front door and her lifeless body dragged into the living-room where she was then dismembered. The pathologist estimated the process of dismemberment would have taken a considerable time, an hour at least.

Cosy had mentioned in his statement that the rattan blinds over the living-room balcony windows were permanently in the open position. This was because they had malfunctioned and would no longer drop. Examination of the blinds revealed that the cord had been cut allowing them to fall into the closed position. It followed that entry to the flat had been made via the insecure living-room balcony window after observing the movements of Samantha within. The perpetrator having gained entry then dropped the blind by cutting the cord to prevent anyone else looking through the window at his devilish work.

The killer having gained access to the flat via the insecure balcony window, at some point disturbed Samantha who confronted him in the hallway. It would appear she had been attacked by an intruder who, on the balance of probabilities, was unlikely to have been known to her.

The meeting concluded and the team went straight back to work. For many, this was a spin around on their chairs to face their desks and making necessary phone calls. Alan spoke to Roger over a cup of tea.

"Well mate this is going to be a sticker."

Roger replied, "I wish Micky hadn't said it was a size 7 shoe. The bloke at forensics said how difficult a print, especially a composite one, was to measure. It depends on the pressure exerted and other factors."

Alan didn't think it of great importance. "At least it has been circulated to check against burglars and that doesn't mention the size." Roger nodded but was still perturbed. He looked tired. He hadn't had a decent night's sleep since being called on 3rd November.

"You know Al. Micky is very worried about this case, he doesn't let on, but it has really got to him."

Alan had an empty feeling, akin to grief. "We'll get there mate. Something will turn up. It always does."

Roger looked pensive. "Well lets see what this bloke Paul Britton comes up with, he should be forwarding a psychological profile soon, apparently its all the rage up at the Yard since that *Cracker* series on TV."

Alan smiled. "I can't see Micky being too impressed."

Police Gazette — Special Notice

DECEMBER 8th 1993

SN 61/93

MURDER

SAMANTHA and JAZMINE BISSET

1

2

MP (RA) · During the morning of 4-11-93 Samantha Bisset, aged 27 years, and her daughter, Jazmine, aged 4 years, were attacked at their home; 1A Heathfield Terrace (L) SE18, receiving serious injuries from which they subsequently died.

It is believed that the suspect (s) were wearing the after-described TRAINING SHOES.

Adidas Phantom Low BASKETBALL SHOES in black with white trim or white with blue trim *(Photograph 1)*, and

Adidas Phantom Mid BASKETBALL SHOES in black with white trim or white with white trim *(photo 2)*.

Any officers with information or who come in contact with persons wearing the above described TRAINING SHOES, please inform Detective Superintendent Banks, Incident Room, Thamesmead Police Station, telephone 081-312 1200.

Police internal appeal notice.

CHAPTER 10

To Scotland

On checking his latest list of actions Alan found he was required to go to Scotland. The bodies had been released from the coroner and were to be buried in Dundee, Margaret Morrison's home town. Several other actions were appended which dealt with visiting old friends of Samantha. Most of these had been established as having known her during her New Age period. They ranged in location from Peterhead down through Aberdeen, Dundee, Arbroath and Edinburgh. None of them were considered a priority but all required a statement and elimination and were also the possible holders, albeit unlikely, of vital information.

Alan arranged a flight to Aberdeen and accommodation at a hotel in Stonehaven. He hired a car from Aberdeen Airport and then planned out the long journey to visit the potential witnesses. He had forewarned all of them, to make sure they would be in when he arrived. Not always the best approach but there were only so many opportunities to knock on a door in Peterhead.

The aeroplane landed on a bleak rainy morning. Complete with road atlas Alan drove southwards from Aberdeen to Stonehaven. He had an appointment that evening with Margaret and Jack Morrison at their house south of Stonehaven. The omens did not feel good when the car burst a tyre shortly after leaving Aberdeen. Alan spent an uncomfortable hour changing the tyre by the roadside in slushy snow. The tyre would have to be replaced, another thing to sort out before driving half-way around Scotland. He arrived at the Royal Hotel just as evening was falling. It was on the sea front, a large Victorian relic which had seen better days. His room gave a view out to the North Sea. The grey waves crashed relentlessly on the beach over a vast bay. There was only just time to shower before leaving for the Morrison's house. He asked at reception about the whereabouts of a local garage to mend the tyre and then headed off. It was almost dark as he turned off the main road to follow a minor one down to the village. Jack's house was easy to find, it was the only one. An assortment of period petrol pumps adorned the drive. Jack was waiting at the door.

The hospitality was overwhelming. Margaret was in the living-room. Alan awkwardly asked how they were and explained he would attend the funeral if that was still their wish. Jack seemed to be in control, and yes, he would want Alan to do so. He then went on to explain in great detail how to find the cemetery and stressed he wanted Alan to attend the reception afterwards. Alan produced from his briefcase the statement forms and took a formal statement from Margaret in which she gave some background to Samantha's life and then formally identified her as the body she had seen at Greenwich mortuary. The sombre meeting took up the best part of two hours before Alan bid them farewell and made his way back along the coast road to his hotel.

The following morning was consumed by getting the tyre repaired. As he paid by cheque Alan wondered what the finance department would think of this one. The rest of the day was a busy schedule travelling up the east coast and visiting people on the list, yellow van owners and acquaintances, hoping they may have something to offer the enquiry. All of them remembered Samantha with affection and admiration but none had any information which could progress the investigation.

Another late night and then it was the day of the funeral. The weather hadn't improved. A gathering of about 30 people were at the church service. The two coffins lay side by side, Jazmine's white. Some of Samantha's favourite music was played as the coffins left the church. Not the most usual of choices and strange enough to raise a few smiles.

Alan followed the hearse to the cemetery at Barnhill and parked in a nearby street, the rain continued its relentless drizzle. A small crowd gathered at the graveside where the coffins were lowered into the ground, first Samantha then Jazmine. Laid together. Margaret was having difficulty keeping her emotions in check and Jack stood next to her, his arm over her shoulder, face impassive.

At the reception Alan spoke briefly to Margaret. Jack took him to one side. "Alan I would like to thank you for all the help you have given." He was taken aback. Firstly he couldn't think of anything he had done to help and muttered something about how he was always available should Jack and Margaret require anything. Then blurted out, "Jack I will do all in my power to find out who did this." It sounded corny, even as he said it.

Jack replied, "I know you will son. You will always be welcome here."

Alan felt a sudden hollow feeling in the pit of his stomach. The enormity of what had happened dawned on him and for the first time in any investigation he had ever been involved in he felt a pang of raw emotion. He shook Jack's hand and left the reception to visit more potential witnesses. None of the people listed had anything to offer which could forward the enquiry, but it took another day to see them all.

On the last day Alan drove back to the Morrisons to say his goodbyes before departing for Aberdeen. The foul weather had lifted slightly giving a glimpse of the glorious countryside and sea views. Scotland in its unbeatable glory. Margaret and Jack made him feel like an old family friend and bid him a safe journey. Alan told them he would be back. He didn't realise in what shocking circumstances that would be.

A ex-GPO van of the kind seen close to the murder scene.

CHAPTER 11

The Investigation Falters

There is nothing worse in a murder investigation than when the point is reached when the leads run dry. The actions continue to churn out, the results of which are sent back through the system in the incident room resulting in more actions. Inevitably, insidiously, the feeling of failure creeps into the team. The daily briefings become twice weekly, then once weekly, as the statements pile up and the actions are crossed off. The initial surge having died away, senior officers start to calculate the cost of keeping the investigation running. One-by-one investigators are pared-off to assist other enquiries.

Christmas had come and gone with nothing to give the team hope. Micky Banks knew the importance of this case and fought his corner hard. He took the time honoured route of applying to have the murders screened on *Crimewatch*. At first the BBC, in common with the rest of the media, showed little interest. Their curiosity was piqued when Micky Banks told them that the clinical psychologist Paul Britton had done a profile. The BBC was only interested if Britton could be persuaded to appear on the programme. Britton, being a very private man, was averse to the idea but relented, so long as he only concentrated on the psychological profile. He agreed to appear and consequently the BBC decided to run it and preparations were made. It is always hoped that because of the popularity of the TV show there may be something generated which would give the team a new lead.

Meanwhile everybody wracked their brains to try and open a different avenue for the enquiry to turn into. Alan had driven over Plumstead Common and as he passed the flat he stopped the car and walked over to 1a Heathfield Terrace. The police "DO NOT CROSS" tape, still preventing access to the steps down to the flat's front door, flapped for-lornly in the bitter January wind. The door itself had been reinforced with a steel, padlocked cover, to prevent any ghoulish sightseers who may be mentally-ill enough to want to see inside. Nobody had been in the flat since the forensic team completed their work in November. Alan walked back up the steps and entered the garden at the rear of the flats. The balcony to 1a was about four feet above ground level. He could see into the living-room where everything stood as it had been left by the police. He had an idea. At the next office meeting he suggested that a fresh look should be taken of the flat. Usually a murder scene will be forensicated and then put back into use when the police have finished with it. In this case it had been left. A small team under the direction of Roger was put together to go through the flat again with a fine toothcomb, to try and find something that would help to carry the investigation forward.

The search took the entire day but at least something was found. Dis-carded in the living-room was a copy of the *Daily Mirror* TV supplement for the first week of November. The magazine was flipped through and on one of the double pages was a faint outline of an Adidas training shoe. This imprint became a vital addition to the composite shoeprint and gave a more definitive shoe size as a size 9. It wasn't much but at least it quietened the continuing confusion over the shoe size being an unlikely size 7.

Banks gave a briefing prior to the *Crimewatch* programme in which he concentrated on the mechanics of the broadcast and how to get the best out of it. He made mention of the psychological profile and acknowl-edged that, without Paul Britton, there wouldn't be a programme. He then gave his views on the profile which Britton had forwarded to the team. "Remember this is not evidence. There is nothing startling about the reasoning and the outcome of the profile. I could have asked any of you to apply your minds to what makes the killer tick and you are all capable of coming up with something to match Mr Britton. It is really common sense."

The night of 8th February 1994 was set for the *Crimewatch* broadcast. Micky Banks with Roger Boydell-Smith and Paul Britton attended the TV studio, the rest of the team manned the telephones in the incident room within the ramshackle environs of Thamesmead Police Station. A TV had been set up to watch the programme. Every telephone in the office was manned ready for the show to go out live.

Micky Banks gave an impassioned appeal including announcing publicly for the first time that Jazmine had been sexually-assaulted. Nick Ross the presenter then introduced Paul Britton who made a plea for the killer to contact him personally. After a few minutes delay the first phone call came in. Then another. For a period of about half-an-hour the phones were all busy and then tailed off to silence at around midnight.

When analysed nothing of great importance had been generated. There was now another long list of van sightings to eliminate. A few names were put forward as suspects without any real reason. No-one called Paul Britton to confess but at least Britton's agreement to assist with the programme resulted in some interest being shown by the press. Subsequent to the *Crimewatch* programme, he played no further part in the Bisset investigation. At least not until a dramatic turn of events.

It is a disadvantage of this type of broadcast that some people will use it as way to annoy or pay back for incidents of personal enmity. However spurious, all calls must be investigated, it is the Law of Sod that when one seemingly unconnected message comes into an incident room, if ignored that is the one that will bite you later.

The piles of messages were converted to actions and the actions resulted in statements or further actions, or were confirmed to be of no relevance.

One caller phoned in on the night to say excitedly, "I know the killer, I know who he is." Enid Lamb one of the indexers took the call.

"Yes sir, who is he?"

"I know him. He's an actor who lives down in Chatham."

"Chatham, yes sir."

"I'm amazed you haven't found out who he is."

It transpired that the caller was talking about the actor who had played the part of the killer in the *Crimewatch* mock up of events.

Enid patiently tried to explain, "Yes, thank you sir, we know he is an actor. He was playing the part for *Crimewatch*."

"Well, why haven't you arrested him then?"

The investigation rumbled on into February and March without any significant breakthrough. Pressure was mounting to scale down the operation. Alan was increasingly feeling the pressure, he had many conversations with Roger and other team members about ways to open up the investigation to a new line of enquiry. Every person with whom Samantha had had contact over the past ten years, her school friends, her New Age associates her local contacts, her contacts made through her advertising in lonely hearts columns. Her modelling photographers were all seen and no connection could be made which would engender the slightest suspicion.

Roger was roped-in to assist with the interviewing of people who had contacted Samantha through the lonely hearts columns. His partner on these forays was Sean McGowan, a young constable on attachment from Peckham Crime Squad, eager to join the CID as a detective. The calls made were carried out as cold calls. This was done to put the person interviewed on the back foot, but did produce some unforeseen reactions.

A visit in Dagenham was to a person identified as having responded to one of Samantha's newspaper messages. The action was handwritten and referred to a Mrs Jones, unusually a female correspondent. Late in the evening Roger and Sean knocked on the door and it was answered by a Mrs Jones. When asked if she had any knowledge of Samantha she replied "No". Some further questions and answers were sallied back and forth until a male voice was heard from within.

"Who is it?"

Mrs Jones called out, "It's the police, asking about a Samantha Bisset."

There was silence. Roger looked more closely at the handwritten action. It actually referred to a "Mr S Jones". No matter how sensitive enquirers try to be, mistakes will be made. Mr Jones had contacted Samantha but had no further involvement. He no doubt had some explanation ready for his wife after Sean and Roger departed.

On another occasion Roger and Sean were instructed to see another correspondent who lived in Suffolk, near Stansted Airport, where he was a helicopter pilot. The door was answered by the man they were looking for. Behind the man Roger could see his wife chopping salad with a large kitchen knife on her chopping board. The lady made her way to the front door to stand by her husband, kitchen knife in hand.

Trying to be sensitive after introducing himself, Roger said "This is a very sensitive enquiry, it may be better if we spoke in the car." The man replied. "That will not be necessary, I have no secrets from my wife."

Roger persisted, "Just maybe we could ask a few questions in private?" The man was adamant his wife be allowed to listen in.

Roger felt he had to dive straight in, "Have you been in correspondence with a lady called Samantha Bisset?" The man reddened with embarrassment, husband and wife looked at each other, the knife weighing in her hand. The interview was concluded in the car and the man was satisfactorily cleared of any involvement. Sean escorted him back to his door where he could see the man's wife, hacking away at the vegetables.

Banks announced at a meeting in April that the squad would be cut down over the next two months. Detective Sergeant Bob Thomas the office manager was retiring on the 22nd April and would not be replaced. Bob was loathe to leave in the middle of an unsolved investigation but with no end to the enquiry in sight decided he would not delay his departure.

Over the next two months the team was cut back relentlessly. By early July all that was left of the investigating team were a uniformed police constable, Mary Salt who had taken over as acting office manager, Detective Inspector Bryan Reeve who took over day to day command of the team and, without any detective sergeants available, Alan was made acting detective sergeant. Roger also remained as exhibits officer/investigator, together with Detective Constable Peter Canavan, Detective Constable Alison Cocklin and the indispensable Pamela Robinson, who managed the indexing and supervision of the now mammoth carousel. They were all that remained of the once 25 strong team.

Prior to being transferred to the Bisset murder team, Pam had been working on the investigation of a series of rapes in south east London into the "Green Chain Walk rapist", so called because all of the offences had been committed along a public footway which traversed south east London parks known as the Green Chain Walk. The investigation's official title was Operation Eccleston. The perpetrator had not been identified and because no new offences had been committed for several months the it had been wound down and closed. The investigation had been looked at as having a possible link to the murders of Samantha and Jazmine. The files were examined for similarities and because all of the rapes bar one had been committed on open public land it was felt unlikely to be by the same offender. In any event, as no person had been identified, despite having a DNA profile of the attacker, it didn't assist the murder enquiry.

The press had again lost all interest. Alan was having sleepless nights. No other job had affected him like this current one. He had always been able to compartmentalise his feelings but now the barriers were being eroded. The sleepless nights were interspersed with frequent nightmares. The dream was always the same: he stood on a foreshore and a ferry was approaching, an old fashioned river-type with just a set of railings around a flat base. The ferry rode up to the shore line and the ramp dropped at the front. There was one person on the ferry who stood at the rear then slowly walked toward where he was waiting on the shore. The figure was hooded and raised its right arm aloft in a beckoning motion. Walking nearer and nearer, off the ferry and then ... Alan woke with a start in a sweat. The dream kept repeating itself and Alan knew it would never cease until this case was resolved.

The office became quieter, the phones rarely rang. The day-to-day routine of completing actions and statements continued. Further research was under way on the Adidas trainer; messages were sent to its country of origin, Korea, trying to narrow down batch numbers and distribution. A trawl was made of all the early messages and statements looking for inconsistencies. Anything.

Long hours were spent visiting hippy camp sites over the south of England and Wales. Anyone who had ever known Samantha was tracked down and interviewed. All of them remembered Samantha as a lively, intelligent woman without enemies. She was inevitably described as being self-assured and someone who would stand her corner.

The day of Alan's yearly attempt at the sergeant's examination at Hendon came and went. He hadn't the time to give up a day wasted at the examination centre at Hendon. In any event any thought of study had long been dismissed as the weight of the Bisset case drove down on his every thought. He knew he should devote some time to studying for the exam, he had in fact passed the wretched thing when he had just over two years in the police but had been told he needed to requalify to stand a chance under the new assessment system.

One afternoon the office was surprised by a visit from Area Detective Chief Superintendent Bill Ilsely. He gathered the small team together in the now spacious Thamesmead office and asked how things were going, DI Reeve wasn't in the office. Alan gave him a précis of latest information. Ilsely, nodded, smiled and looked about the room.

He then said, "Well do you think we will solve this?"

There was a moment of silence, Bill's face traversed from face-to-face. Alan suddenly felt this was a moment of importance. Bill Ilsley was here to judge for himself the worth of continuing the enquiry. Alan drew a deep breath.

"Yes sir absolutely, we still have avenues of enquiry. We are determined to find the killer. Not only that, but it is imperative we do. This man will kill again."

Ilsely continued smiling and replied. "Good answer. Well, carry on." He left the office and the team watched as he drove out of the car park and through the wire fence gate onto the Thamesmead estate. Peter Canavan, clutching a mug of tea said, "You are such a bloody creep Al. But he's right it's a good answer."

Alan looked up from his desk. "I meant it Pete."

POLICE APPEAL FOR ASSISTANCE

RAPE

A number of sex attacks have happened in this area predominantly on open ground. The suspect is described as a white male, aged 19-30 years, 5'7" - 5'9" tall, athletic build, pale complexion, brown lank hair. Usually wearing a black leather jacket, white T-shirt and baggy blue jeans. He may carry a knife.

HAVE YOU SEEN THIS MAN?
DO YOU KNOW HIM?
CAN YOU HELP?
Please contact the Incident Room at
ELTHAM POLICE STATION
TEL: 081•294 1361

METROPOLITAN
POLICE

All information
treated as strictly
confidential

OR RING

CRIMESTOPPERS
0800 555 111

Green Chain Walk rapes appeal poster.

CHAPTER 12

A Breakthrough

Micky Banks had thrashed out every possible direction the enquiry might take. He had long discussions with Bryan Reeve on how much longer he could keep the enquiry alive. He was open to every suggestion coming in from the team. Every aspect of the investigation was revisited, again-and-again. The feeling was, there must be something. Studying the forensic schedule he remarked to Bryan, "Have you ever seen a job where every fingerprint is eliminated from a crime scene?"

Bryan replied, "No Guvnor, it is a bit odd. Even the prints from all the children at Jazmine's party were identified." Micky looked again at the fingerprint schedule. "Let's arrange an interview with Derek Phillips, see what he says about it." Derek was heading the fingerprint section responsible for the Bisset murders. A meeting was hastily arranged for him to attend Thamesmead to discuss the fingerprint evidence. Even over the phone he showed his reluctance. But the next day he duly arrived and went into conference with Micky Banks. He was adamant that all fingerprints had been scrutinised. He detailed how the procedure was carried out.

After taking fingerprints from a scene, known as "lifts" (so called because they are literally lifted from where they are found using adhesive tape) they are then examined by an expert who will identify them or not against the criminal records of all known criminals. This is a skilled and laborious process. Once the fingerprints have been examined, before a result can be recorded, they are double-checked by another independent expert. Phillips was sure that no mistake could have been made. It is well-known no two sets of fingerprints can be identical. This has been established in criminal law for over 100 years, since 1900 when intro-duced by Home Secretary Richard Henry.

Banks requested that all the fingerprints be looked at again. Phillips wasn't keen, this was an expensive exercise and he was short staffed as it was. Banks was insistent and Phillips against his better judgement agreed to run them again. The news was relayed back into the main office at the meeting held afterwards. Not much hope was held out by anyone. It would be different if there were some outstanding prints, but there seemed little mileage in re-running prints which had already been identified.

Within a couple of days a rumour spread within the team. There was something not right about the fingerprints. Banks was in early and Phillips had been summoned to Thamesmead. The team gathered in the main office. The date was 20ᵗʰ May 1994. Bryan sat impassively and would not be drawn. Only a gruff, "Let the guvnor have his chat with Derek Phillips."

Something was definitely up, the tension was high in the air, cups of tea were brewed and forgotten. At last through the side door the suited Phillips appeared. He was carrying a briefcase in his right hand. Bank's office was directly in front of him. Bryan rose to his feet and opened the office door. Phillips smiled again and the hushed office heard him pro-nounce, "Another great day for fingerprint branch." He said this loudly enough for even Bryan to hear and it carried into the main office. The room fell silent as Bryan took his seat. After a few moments raised voices could be heard coming from Banks' office.

"No … It isn't a triumph it's a bloody disgrace." A few more words were exchanged and Phillips left. Without a pause, he exited the police station for the car park. There was a further full two minutes silence as eyes played on Banks' office door. Eventually it opened, Micky appeared smoking a roll-up. Very calm, suit immaculate, tie firmly in place.

"Right Bryan, office meeting. Is everyone here."

The small group clustered together. Alan felt butterflies in his stomach, whatever was about to happen was going to prove sensational. Banks didn't sit. "I have just spoken to Derek Phillips from fingerprints. It appears that some problem has happened over the results. Phillips tells me that some of the fingerprints have been mis-identified and there has been confusion over some of the victim's fingerprints."

The atmosphere could be cut with a knife.

Banks continued in his calm voice. "There are three prints, one on the balcony, one on the door jam to Jazmine's bedroom and one on the cot of Jazmine which we were told belonged to the victim." He paused and looked slowly round the office. The atmosphere in the scruffy room was electric. "I am told that the patterns were so similar as to make identification difficult and it was assumed without a proper double-check that they belonged to Samantha. Another pause while Banks dragged on his roll-up. "They do not belong to Samantha ... They belong to a man called Robert Napper."

A sudden buzz swept the office.

"I will be recalling a full team to assist. In the meantime, research Napper. I want to know everything about him. Do not let this information go beyond this office."

Micky and Bryan left the incident room together and disappeared into Micky Banks' office, the door closed behind them. The remainder of the gathering, after a moment of shock, suddenly galvanised into action. Checks were made and Napper was found to be a local man who had previous convictions. Whilst a Criminal Records Office (CRO) check was requested Alan phoned the collator at Plumstead Police Station.

"Yes," they did have a record on Napper and "yes", there was a photograph. Alan rushed out into the yard, jumped into his car and sped down to Plumstead Police Station where the collator was waiting with the card on Robert Napper. Stuffing a card signed by himself into the gap left by the Napper card showing the original out at Thamesmead murder incident room, Alan then sped back to Thamesmead. Within 40 minutes Alan was back in the office with the photograph and collators record.

Alan looked at the photo. It was of a young white male in his early-twenties, short greasy hair, spotty complexion and weak chin, staring at the camera with washed-out blue eyes. Nobody recognised him. Pam Robinson the cheerful indexer suddenly piped up with an enthusiastic voice, "That's the Green Chain rapist." At first everyone thought she had just made a poor joke. But the seriousness on her face told a different story. "I'm telling you, it's a ringer for the Photofit."

Alan rushed from the room and out into the reception office. The constable on duty was amazed as he vaulted the "jump" and studied a picture which was appended to the wall. There, on a typical Metropolitan Police notice board was a poster seeking information for the identity of the Green Chain Rapist. Underneath a Photofit was the wording. "Have you seen this Man?" The Photofit was of a young white male with a spotty complexion.

Alan ripped it from the wall and leaped back over the jump, swinging his legs within inches of the startled station officer. He stormed into the office and presented it in front of Pam. The photograph from the collator's card was placed next to it. Pam was right. It was a ringer.

It was six months and 16 days since the murder of Samantha and Jazmine Bisset.

CHAPTER 13

Who is Robert Napper?

The greatest fear of a long-running investigation which eventually achieves a breakthrough is that the name of the suspect will have been in the investigation all the time and the investigators have missed it, whether through stupidity, incompetence or mistake. Not only can this be embarrassing in the extreme, it can also be career ending for a murder detective.

In a case such as Samantha and Jazmine there was the added fear that whilst the team were running around in circles, the offender was committing offences elsewhere. All the indicators from profiling experts indicated this was not a one off offence, rather it was indicative of a deep-rooted need of a severely psychologically disturbed person, and the offender would strike again. There was always a queue at New Scotland Yard of senior officers who had no knowledge of the enquiry eager to find some detective somewhere to hang out to dry whilst basking in the glow of hindsight. The carousel card index at the Thamesmead murder incident room, which contained the names of every person who had ever entered the enquiry, was searched and showed no reference, not even obliquely to Napper.

Within a day most of the original team had rejoined the squad. Napper had been found to be living at an address in Plumstead High Street, No. 135 and a surveillance squad was hastily put together to keep observations on his movements. The property was of the Victorian Terrace-type and had been split into bedsits. The time of year now being mid-May the long hours of daylight gave plenty of opportunity for Napper to strike again, even as the team consolidated all the information they could find on him. It was tempting to arrest him immediately but so much information was now streaming into the incident room Banks took the decision to hold off the arrest and set up a 24 hour observation on Napper.

Robert Napper's criminal record file was drawn and his previous convictions made interesting reading. By no means could he be described as a habitual criminal and had no convictions for anything of a sexual nature. He had been convicted in August 1986 at Bexley Magistrates' Court of carrying a loaded air weapon in a public place for which he was given a conditional discharge for 12 months. This was his first recorded offence, committed when he was 20-years-old.

Napper's obvious fascination with weapons and firearms continued, on the 2nd December 1992 he was convicted at Woolwich Magistrates' Court of possession of a firearm and ammunition without a certificate, a far more serious and worrying offence, for which he was sentenced to eight weeks imprisonment. The circumstances of this arrest were astonishing and had far reaching consequences. In 1992 Napper was living in Reidhaven Road, Plumstead. Police at Plumstead were informed that an odd character had visited a printing shop called Jetsam Press in Plumstead High Street and had ordered 50 A4 size letter headings of the Metropolitan Police logo and crest with the wording Greenwich Division printed underneath. Police waited at the shop and a man who was later identified as Robert Napper appeared. When police approached Napper he ran off but was quickly caught and arrested. Suspicions being aroused, police searched his address at No. 63 Reidhaven Road. In the house they found a .22 Erma pistol together with 200 rounds of ammunition, a crossbow, a quantity of knives, a listening device and what was described as a quantity of correspondence which later proved to contain a London *A to Z* street map within which were various hand drawn markings and routes.

The investigating officers charged Napper with possession of a firearm and ammunition without a certificate. Crucially they did not see the importance of the *A to Z* and its link to the currently ongoing Green Chain rapes investigation at Eltham. Furthermore it wasn't current practice at that time to routinely take DNA samples from those charged with criminal offences. After serving 25 days' imprisonment at Belmarsh Prison, Napper was free to fall back into his life of mayhem and murder.

No further offences had been recorded until on 1st February 1994 he was convicted at Woolwich Magistrates' Court of shoplifting for which he received a one year conditional discharge. This was three months after the Bisset murders.

Apart from his previous convictions Napper had a "collator's card" at Plumstead. The card index was kept at police stations of persons coming to notice in the area of that particular police station. Quite apart from his convictions it recorded all other arrests and times when the subject came into the spectrum of "interest" to police. The card on Napper made very interesting reading, especially one entry when police had been called to a possible "Peeping Tom" in Rutherglen Road, Abbeywood on the night of Saturday 31st August 1993 at 9.30 pm.

Rutherglen Road is within a mile of where Napper was living in Plumstead High Street and close to Winns Common. It backs onto the Green Chain Walk and an open grassland area. Behind the houses in the road are a row of hedges and trees. On that Saturday evening one of the house occupiers noticed a male climbing a wall at the rear of the houses, he appeared to be holding either a knife or a screwdriver and seemed to be staring into the rear of his next door neighbour's house. The witness turned on his powerful outside garden light and watched as the man jumped down and retreated back into the bushes. Whatever he was carrying in his right hand he tucked inside his jacket. The witness called the police. The neighbour concerned was a young woman in her twenties. She was described as slim and blond.

The informant kept observation on the man and, as the police arrived saw him run off. Police searched the area and in a nearby alleyway which gave access to garages Special Constable Abbot using his torch found Napper. He stood out because he was wearing white training shoes. He called for his sergeant using his police radio and Sergeant William Bienick arrived. He was searched and nothing like a knife or screwdriver was found. Sergeant Bienick questioned Napper and found him rather odd. Napper answered his questions in a peculiarly stilted manner, at one point answering. "I wasn't moving. I have not committed a moving traffic violation." No offences were disclosed and Napper was taken back to his address in Plumstead High Street. Bienick was disturbed enough by the incident and Napper's behaviour to make a lengthy entry in the stop and search form. He described Napper as quiet and withdrawn but then went on to note he was a man capable of extreme violence who should be considered for any future rape or indecency offences. The murder of Samantha and Jazmine was to happen just over two months later.

The final entry in the collator's system at Plumstead was one by PC Troon which concerned Napper's arrest for shoplifting £6.09 worth of confectionary from Kwiksave in Plumstead High Street on 10th January 1994 at 8.35 am, two months after the murder. Napper was described as six feet tall, slim build, eleven stone, mousy scruffy hair and with a spotty complexion. He was wearing blue jeans, a dark tracksuit top and trainers. He was also described as being softly spoken and cooperative but at times appeared to be daydreaming. The height given of six feet would prove significant.

Whilst observations were being kept, the background of Napper was being filled-in quickly. He had been born and raised locally by his parents Pauline and Brian Napper. He was the eldest of four children having one sister and two brothers. The marriage was not a happy one, Napper's father was of a violent disposition and so it appeared would often assault his wife both mentally and physically. Allegedly, the abuse was regularly carried out in the presence of the children who were afraid of him. Robert Napper attended Blackfen Primary School where he was described as being reticent to mix with other children and had a habit of shutting himself away. At one point his mother was summonsed to the school as Robert had been caught stealing from other children.

In 1976 Napper's mother was admitted to Queen Mary's Hospital Woolwich with a kidney complaint. During this two week period her four children were fostered out by social services. It was during 1976 that the marriage failed completely and a divorce was granted in December of that year when Robert Napper was ten-years-old.

Napper's father Brian allegedly continued to plague the family, despite the divorce and would turn up at the family home and be abusive and threatening to Pauline Napper. The children were so traumatised by this that they were admitted to the Maudsley Psychiatric Hospital for counselling. Pauline took on the arduous duty of transporting them there by public transport once a week. Napper's siblings responded to treatment and were discharged but Robert continued with his treatment until the age of 16 years.

Respite was achieved from Brian Napper when in 1980 he remarried and emigrated to Australia. Robert Napper left school without any academic qualifications in the summer of 1982 and went on to take up various employments in the catering trade. In 1985 he worked at a wine bar called *El Vino's* in Martin Lane, Cannon Street where he was employed as a kitchen assistant. After working there for two years, in 1987 he found work locally in Felixstowe Road, Abbey Wood, London SE2 with a company known as Davu Wire where he worked as "cable operator" on night shifts.

In March of 1989 Napper was employed by the Palace of Westminster as an under-chef. Enquiries at the palace revealed he had difficulty "fitting in" as one manager described it. It came as no surprise to anyone when he left this employment one month later. Napper continued to fall in-and-out of employment until, in November of 1989 he was employed by Serco. Serco was a company contracted to the Ministry of Defence to carry out building work at the vast Royal Arsenal site in Woolwich SE28. The work involved the management and storage of forms used within the MOD organization. The sprawling site was virtually defunct by this time but was still out of bounds to the general public. Within its fences and walls were many crumbling fine Georgian buildings linked by a network of virtually unused roads. During its heyday the site had employed tens of thousands of ammunition workers. Napper was employed there as a storesman. His responsibilities were to deal with large quantities of forms for the MOD. He continued at this work from 1989 through to 1992 when in September he was made redundant as a result of the Arsenal site being completely shut down and earmarked for re-development. Napper was paid £3,400 in redundancy money.

Enquiries with Serco showed that Napper was viewed as a loner, some of the staff describing him as "weird" and stating he would often talk to himself. He was especially uncommunicative to the female staff who were wary of him. His time-keeping was erratic but generally he was a good worker. After being made redundant by Serco, Napper remained unemployed up to and beyond the murder of Samantha and Jazmine in November 1993.

On 4th February 1994, two-and-a half months after the murder, and immediately after his shoplifting conviction, Napper obtained employment at Glyndon Plastics Thamesmead. This factory was situated about 20 minutes walk from his address in Plumstead High Street. It was day work beginning at 8 am and finishing at 8 pm. The tasks he was given were of a low grade nature which he had no problems performing, however, as in all previous employments, his time-keeping was erratic and he took days off sick and didn't follow company guidelines to call in giving the reason for his absence. Napper was spoken to by his supervisor about this and did not take kindly to being admonished, greeting it with a sullen silence. The familiar pattern of problems with female staff arose and their fear of him.

On the week of 16th May 1994, Alan found himself on observation duty over the main entrance to 135 Plumstead High Street noting the comings and goings of someone he was getting to know. Napper kept to a rigid routine in the mornings. Always leaving his bedsit via the front door at 7 am. He turned right on the High Street towards Woolwich and first right again into Bannockburn Road, then took the direct route to the Thamesmead Trading Estate.

CHAPTER 14

The Pre-arrest

From the day Napper's fingerprints had been identified Pam Robinson and fellow indexer Jane Stutchbury were vociferous in their suspicions that Napper was responsible for the Green Chain Walk rapes. Micky Banks and Bryan Reeve did not need much convincing and the lead officers from the now defunct Green Chain Rape enquiry were asked to attend Thamsmead for a conference. The last recorded rape attack, which had been particularly violent, had been in King John's Walk, Eltham SE9 on the 15th July 1992.

The two officers, Det Supt Steve Landeryou and DI John Pearse who had been in charge of the investigation named Operation Eccleston attended. On arrival they were immediately ensconced in Micky Banks' tiny office. DS Landeryou was an old time detective. Always immaculately dressed in a dark three piece suit which was topped-off by a gold chain strung neatly across his waistcoat, he had been involved in some high profile cases in the past, although it was in the long distant past. He lived off the memories of past glories and fostered the image; he was I believe uncomfortably close to the press at times, some of whom bought into that image. Landeryou it is believed had been keen to run down Operation Eccleston and consign the enquiry to the dusty shelves of records at New Scotland Yard.

John Pearse was cut from different cloth. Young, ambitious and forceful, he was the driving force behind the Eccleston enquiry. It had become a thorn in his side. He was typical of the new breed of detective, he had a deep-rooted interest in the causes of crime and the psychology of the criminal. When not at his day job he was studying for a Phd in criminal psychology. Operation Eccleston had been an ideal project for him to get his teeth into. A series of progressively more violent rapes committed in a small area of urban London. The study, without a culprit, seemed to be turning into a hypothetical exercise.

Together with Bryan Reeve the four officers crammed into Micky Banks' office. All knew what was on the agenda, all had a different perspective. Banks knew Steve Landeryou well and the two were not on close terms. Banks opened the conversation.

"You know why you are here, it seems at last we have a suspect for our murder. This bloke Robert Napper. No previous for sexual offences as far as we can tell. However his Photofit, his odd personality, the fact he knows the local area so well makes us believe he may be the Green Chain rapist."

Landeryou replied, "Well it's a theory I suppose."

John Pearse cut in. "We have checked our HOLMES computer. The name Napper does come in and he was seen. But he was eliminated."

Banks' bushy eyebrows rose. "How was he eliminated?"

If Pearse was worried he didn't show it.

"All of the descriptions given were of a suspect who was 5' 7" to 5' 8" tall. Napper was 6' 1". He was eliminated on the height parameters."

Banks sat back unfazed, "I understand you have good DNA evidence on your job. Was Napper ever blood tested?"

An intake of breath from Steve Landeryou.

Pearse ploughed on confidently. "We had a couple of messages into the system putting Napper up as resembling the Photofit. He was contacted and asked to come into Eltham police station to give blood."

A moment's silence.

"And?" said Banks. John Pearse continued. "We hadn't had an offence for some considerable time. We were closing-down the enquiry on instructions from above. We made an assessment based on the description and as he was described as being over 6' tall, it wasn't pursued."

Another silence.

Micky continued, "So, let's get this straight. He was identified by the Photofit and asked to come in to give blood?"

The two Eccleston officers nodded.

Landeryou said, "As you know, Photofits are notoriously unreliable. The officers who visited him reported he was far too tall."

Banks continued. "He failed to attend to give a blood sample and was written off on height description?" Nods from the Eccleston quarter.

"Without going into great detail, how many times was he identified as being like the Photofit?" Landeryou looked at Pearse who said, "Twice"

"And how many times was he asked to come in to give blood?"

Pearse again said, "Twice." The uncomfortable atmosphere continued. Banks spoke, "Well gentlemen, we will be arresting Napper soon. On his arrest a DNA sample will be taken. Then we will know one way or the other. In the meantime Mr Ilsley has authorised the reopening of the Eccleston account. I suggest you make sure that it is all up to date."

Banks looked at each officer pointedly. "Let's hope Napper isn't your man. But I've got to say … it does look like it."

Pearse chipped in breezily. "I am confident we have made the right decision and Napper is not the Green Chain rapist." Landeryou looked less sure. "Whatever the outcome we can show we have done everything possible." Landeryou and Pearse left the office and sped off to Eltham to re-open Operation Eccleston. This was good advice for, even though the enquiry had officially been "closed down" there were many actions left unresolved.

A search was made of the files at Plumstead Police Station and Roger found a reference in the property store to items seized when Napper had been arrested for possession of a firearm and ammunition in December of 1992. A check with the property store and what was filed under "Other correspondence" revealed an *A to Z* street map of London which had been used by Napper. It was taken back to Thamesmead where it was more closely examined. There were many hand drawn marks within the pages, apparently describing jogging routes, and various doodles. The most obvious fact in common to the majority of the marks was that they were all on sections of the Green Chain Walk and even more significantly in places where Green Chain rape offences had taken place. Steve Landeryou and John Pearse were asked to revisit Thamesmead and were updated with the latest findings.

The approaching weekend was a bank holiday. The number of officers on the enquiry team had suddenly more than quadrupled. A surveillance team followed Napper's every move. Their reports showed some disturbing behaviour. The surveillance started on Friday 20th May. They confirmed that Napper did reside at 135 Plumstead High Street. He was employed at Glyndon Plastics in Nathan Way where he did a 12 hour shift from 8 am to 8 pm from Monday to Friday.

The next day, Saturday, Napper was on his day off and making the most of it. After leaving his home address at 1.21 pm and visiting local shops he boarded a BR train to Charing Cross. Upon arrival at Charing Cross he was seen entering a sportswear shop and then a newsagents where he browsed the top shelf for sex magazines and eventually purchased two of them. He then picked up a magazine entitled *Guns and Ammo* which he examined without buying. After this he entered a camping equipment shop where he showed a keen interest in the combat knives.

Whilst on his travels he carried a black Jaguar sports bag, and was wearing a mustard yellow-coloured hooded coat, blue jeans and black shoes. One further telling report from the surveillance describes Napper as walking with a pronounced stoop. He was described by the surveillance team as being about 5' 10" tall instead of his true height of almost 6' 2".

On Sunday the 21st of May Napper was again on his travels. He was carrying his black Jaguar sports bag. After several short bus journeys locally, he boarded a train at Woolwich. He changed trains at Blackheath and again travelled up to Charing Cross. There he made a bee line for W H Smith the newsagents and crouched down at the rear of the shop to peruse without purchasing *Guns and Ammo* magazine. He walked onto The Strand and entered confectioners where he purchased two sex magazines, then walked to a camping shop where he studied their selection of camping/hunting knives.

Late on the evening of Tuesday the 24th of May at 8.50 pm Napper was seen to leave his address dressed in dark clothing and a black baseball cap, he appeared to be training and moved quickly, striding out to St Nicholas Road about a half mile from his address before turning around and returning home. This activity really did put the wind up the enquiry team. Half-term was approaching the following week. Napper was out training, he had shown interest in sex magazines, knives and guns. The dreaded possibility was that he was about to strike again. An emergency office meeting was called. The regular team members assembled at Plumstead Police Station where they were given a debriefing of the latest surveillance. To be nervous was not in Banks' nature. He puffed relentlessly at his roll-up cigarette. Without further ado he addressed the team.

"We cannot risk letting this go on for any longer. We will arrest Napper on Friday morning. Bryan, clear it with Bexleyheath, we will take him there, they have better facilities than Plumstead and also have installed a video interview room which we will utilise. Alan," Micky looked directly over at Alan who was standing with notebook in hand, "I want you to put together the arrest team. Bear in mind he has previous for firearm offences." Alan could only think to himself how pleased he was that after seven months this investigation was finally coming to a head.

Micky continued: "Bryan, you and Pete Canavan will do the interview, we will have a representative from the Eccleston enquiry here and they will conduct their own interview after ours. I have been in touch with the criminal psychologist Paul Britton. He has agreed to assist us and will supervise the interviews." Banks' eyes looked up briefly towards the ceiling. He was as big a fan of psychological profiling as he was computer technology. As good as a confession that Britton's presence had been imposed from above. "He will be here to assist and advise, he will not take part in the interview."

"Roger, you will take charge of the search of Napper's flat once he has been arrested."

"Yes guv," Roger replied.

"Finally, keep this under your hats. We don't want any leaks or any possibility that Napper may get the wind up. The surveillance will continue up to the arrest and naturally should he look like he may attack, they will step in." The meeting concluded late that night, a quiet excitement buzzed around the office. Alan thought again to himself, could this really be happening, seven months of work could be blown in one mishap, one oversight.

On Thursday evening a final briefing had been scheduled at Plumstead Police Station. The entire CID office had been commandeered. The office filled and at 7 pm Micky Banks addressed the gathering. The surveillance team were there, apart from two officers who were monitoring Napper's address. He had been seen to enter his flat earlier, much earlier than his usual 8.30 pm after work. He had not been seen to re-emerge. Also in the briefing room was an officer who was in charge of a "body dog", one trained in the detection of dead bodies in the hope that the missing piece of Samantha's flesh might be in the flat. There were communication staff and all of the investigation team. Next to Bryan Reeve sat John Pearse.

Banks spoke, the 30 or so officers listened. He repeated his instructions of Tuesday evening only going into greater detail. Alan knew he would be called upon to give his briefing in a moment. He had been told that the arrest would be made outside the bedsit as Napper made his way to work. The reason for this was that Napper had a serious firearm offence conviction and showed an interest in knives and guns. It was highly unlikely he would be carrying weapons on his way to work. Secondly, surveillance had been unable to establish exactly where in the house Napper lived. A decision had been made not to approach the landlord or any other occupier in case Napper was tipped off. It was believed the flat was on the first floor.

At the end of his briefing Banks went around the room and asked all individuals what their brief was. Each officer responded. Alan sat at the far end. His notes ready.

"Alan?"

Alan felt the eyes upon him, a briefing to an audience larger than what he was used to. He looked down the table and directed his address to Micky Banks.

"The issue which makes this arrest different from the run of the mill is the fact of the suspect's previous convictions for serious firearm offences. Surveillance has not been able to identify exactly where in 135 Plumstead High Street Napper has his bedsit and it has been agreed that it is too risky to approach any other members of the household at this stage. What we do know is that Napper is a creature of habit, he leaves for work on foot each morning at 7 am. He has always taken the same route, turning right out of his address and then taking the first right into Bannockburn Road. I will wait at the corner of the High Street with DC Canavan and DC Johnstone. Just in case he decides to be different and turns left, two officers will be stationed at the junction of High Street and Kashgar Road. The front door will be under surveillance and we will be informed immediately when he emerges from his front door and whether he turns right or left. Whichever way he turns, we will converge and arrest him."

All were listening.

"Once arrested and after a brief search for any weapons he may be carrying he will be taken back to 135 and his bedsit. The bedsit will then be searched under Section 18 PACE. Arrangements have been made for a police van from Bexleyheath to transport him to Bexleyheath Police Station to be booked in."

Alan paused, that was it, keep it simple. Banks remained silent and Alan waited for him to indicate the next person to take his turn.

"I don't agree with that." All eyes turned to DI John Pearse who continued, "This arrest must go without a hitch, the rest of the investigation depends upon it. We should introduce an outer cordon of officers, what if Napper attempts to make a run for it? We should include in that cordon a dog unit. We should consider the use of India 99." (The police helicopter). There was a stunned silence. Alan looked down at what now appeared to be his rather feeble notes. Pearse sat, upright, seemingly flushed, with a look of triumph on his face. Eyes swung to Banks, this was an unexpected, interesting departure from the norm.

Banks did not look at Pearse who sat immediately to his left, but directly at Alan. It appeared he had been as taken aback as everyone else. Alan started to feel uncomfortable.

"Alan …" he paused running the situation through his head. "Are you satisfied with the plan you have put forward?" If ever there was a moment of truth this was it. Alan knew he had to be positive. He thought to himself. "Don't give an inch." He spoke up with more gusto than he felt inside. "It is a perfectly good plan. This may be a high profile job, but at the end of the day it's a straightforward arrest like any other."

Banks allowed himself a smile, his hands were laid in front of him on the table. "Right, we will go with your plan then."

Alan felt a surge of relief.

Banks looked sideways at Pearse then again down the table at Alan. "But, if it all goes pear-shaped, it will be your fault."

This was greeted with a chuckle of laughter from the assembly, though Alan didn't see the funny side of it. He tried to concentrate on the rest of the briefing but couldn't help but wonder. "John Pearse? What was that about? Why didn't he say anything before the briefing started? Does he know something I don't."

Eventually the briefing was brought to a close. It was late. Alan called his small arrest team around him for a few brief words before the morrow, and they arranged to meet at Plumstead at 6 am before departing for home and a sleepless night.

CHAPTER 15

Going Pear-shaped

It was well after midnight before Alan eventually got home and to bed. He set the alarm for 5.20 am eventually managing some fitful sleep before, all too soon, the alarm bell rang. His thoughts immediately switched to the arrest. He quickly dressed into his old "clobber" as he referred to it, jeans, loose walking jacket, walking boots. No time for tea, he grabbed his watch and warrant card from the hallway windowsill and went out into the fresh May morning air. The weather promised to be fine, the early morning sun was already shining on the branches of the oak trees in the woods opposite, they were at last sprouting their greenery after a long winter. "Always the last to show." He climbed into the old Fiesta and fired up first go. A good sign.

The roads to Plumstead Police Station were clear, it was still too early for most people to start their morning journeys to work. He would normally drive down to Woolwich and along the riverside to Plumstead but this morning, as he had a few minutes to spare, he drove up and over Plumstead Common and on to the adjoining Winns Common where in the kind early light he could see Heathfield Terrace. He stopped very briefly and looked across at No. 1a. Stark in its concrete impassiveness.

"This is what it's all been about Samantha, good morning."

This tendency to chat to the deceased had become more of a habit of late and had intensified as the investigation had progressed. He wondered whether it was a sign, or maybe a first clue of the onset of madness. He recalled early on in the first or second week of the enquiry how Micky Banks had mentioned to the team at the end of an office meeting that if anybody required it there was counselling available. Banks had said it in an almost embarrassed vein, probably resulting from directives above.

Glances were exchanged by those present followed by a low chuckle. Micky Banks had brought the meeting back to order by shrugging his shoulders and exclaiming, "Well. It's there if you want it." As far as Alan was aware no-one had taken up the offer.

The old Fiesta trundled down Riverdale Road and it was obvious he would never be able to park in the station yard. Cars were already parked in all the spaces up the hill and he recognised some of the faces making their way down towards the police station. He squeezed the old banger into a space and walked down to the station yard where he had arranged to meet the arrest team. None of his team were outside the back door as yet, it was still too early. Using his pass he entered the custody door and made his way up to the CID office. It was buzzing with chatter and people. In the corner stood Bryan Reeve and he made his way over towards him.

"Any updates Guvnor?" he asked.

"No," Bryan replied. "Surveillance has him in the house. We will be monitoring you on the radio. Just let me know as soon as he is nicked."

Bryan looked over his glasses. He was relaxed amid the hubbub of the last minute preparations of the office. Micky Banks stood by a white board, he was in conversation with John Pearse. Alan didn't disturb him, he turned to Bryan. "I'll get the radios sorted out and get my team together. I will be in position at 6.30."

Bryan looked up again. "Yeah, good luck, radio in when you are ready."

Alan clattered down the stairs to find his team gathering in the yard. Extra radios had been brought in to cover the operation and the team went into an improvised operations room where they were all issued with one radio apiece. Each officer carried a police issue Asp (a collapsible steel truncheon). After a quick radio check and a final short briefing to ensure everyone knew their part, they made their way out of the back gate and walked down to Plumstead High Street in two small groups. The first two officers stopped at Kashgar Road. Alan said, "Keep yourselves tucked away until I give the word."

He walked on with Peter Canavan and DC Johnstone and passed No. 135 where Napper was hopefully readying himself for work. The front door seemed to beckon. They stopped at the junction with Bannockburn

Road and waited. The weather stayed clear and the temperature was starting to rise.

Alan called in on his radio to operational control at Plumstead. A disembodied voice replied, "Received, we have you in sight." This referred to the observation point which was monitoring the address.

A few people were now moving about in the High Street, one or two gave them brief glances and went on their way. Alan checked his watch as the minute hand approached 7 am. The tension was building. Any moment now Napper would appear from No. 135 and walk towards them. The hand passed the hour mark and continued slowly towards ten minutes past. Nobody came out of the house. Daylight was now absolute but Alan felt a chill. Impatience was showing from the control point.

"Any sign yet?"

"No, nothing yet."

Jokes started to be exchanged between the arrest team about Napper not being in the house. Alan started to have a thought, what if Napper knows he is about to be arrested? What if he is primed and waiting for them instead of the other way around?

The time ticked on. It was now 7.30 am and still no sign of Napper. Alan was feeling restless. Something needed to be done. He radioed in.

"Nobody has emerged from 135. Shall I try a knock on the door?"

There was a silence on the radio for a few moments, then Banks' distinctive voice could be heard.

"Give it five more minutes then go to the door."

Alan looked up, "Did you hear that?" the other two nodded.

Alan turned to Peter Canavan.

"Pete, walk down to the other guys and make sure they know to follow us in in five minutes if he hasn't appeared." Peter nodded and walked down to the next junction. Alan watched as he walked past 135 and in less than two minutes returned. Peter nodded. Alan watched as the five minutes came and went. He thought, "Two extra minutes for things to settle." Two minutes passed and he radioed in. "Arrest team now approaching the HA."

"Received."

He then walked out into the High Street and down towards No. 135.

The team formed up behind him as he climbed the steps to the large imposing front door. There was no bell and he rapped loudly on the woodwork with his knuckles. He watched the front windows for any sign of movement. There was none.

He was expecting a wait but within seconds he could hear someone at the door, sliding a bolt on the inside. It swung open to reveal a young man, dressed in a vest and tracksuit bottoms and carrying a bathroom bag. Whoever he was, Alan could instantly see it wasn't Robert Napper. Alan flashed his warrant card. "Police." He put his finger to his lips to indicate to the man that silence was required. The man looked over Alan's shoulder taking in the sight of five further burly men waiting on the steps.

Alan said quietly, "Which room belongs to Robert Napper?"

The man replied. "I don't know that name, but a man called Rob lives there." With his free hand he pointed to a door about ten yards down the hallway on the left.

Alan replied, "Thank you, now if you wouldn't mind standing aside."

The man retreated back towards the end of the hallway and began to go up the stairs.

The doorway to the room indicated was flimsily made. Alan put his ear to it. There was only silence.

He looked back to see all of his team were at the main doorway.

He gently tried the door handle. It was locked. He looked back at his team. They stood watching him. No smiles or jokes now. He thought, "Oh well, enough pussyfooting around." He gently tested the door for weakness, if it was necessary to force it, a boot aimed at the lock is far better than the shoulder. The shoulder is no good at these moments, if the door doesn't give it really hurts.

Peter Canavan stood next to Alan. He quietly imitated knocking on the door with a clenched fist and looked quizzically at Alan. At Alan's nod Peter tapped on the door. After a short pause it was opened slightly, Alan immediately recognised Napper from the police photograph and with Peter pushed into the room. His senses were at a heightened level, trying to take everything in, in one moment. Napper was naked with the exception of a pair of boxer shorts. Maintaining the initiative Alan stepped over and took his arm, there was no doubt in his mind, the face although in shock, was a mirror image of the police photograph. This was Robert Napper.

Peter Canavan said, "Police, just do as you are told."

Napper stood in shock as DC Johnstone stepped forward and applied handcuffs to him, pinning his arms behind his back. Alan indicated to the other officers to remain in the hallway.

The room was small but well kept and clean, there was no bed, only a mattress on the floor where Napper had obviously been sleeping. Alan stood directly in front of him ensuring they had eye contact. He said, "I am Detective Sergeant Jackaman, I am arresting you for the murders of Samantha and Jazmine Bisset of 1a Heathfield Terrace, Winns Common on the 3rd or 4th November 1993. The grounds for this arrest are forensic evidence. You are not obliged to say anything unless you wish to do so. Anything you say may be given in evidence. Do you understand?" It all sounded very formal but cases have been lost on the simplest examples of disregard for procedure. Napper was still in shock although he had recovered some of his composure. He replied, "Yes."

Alan continued, "In addition we have grounds to suspect, because of your description and what we know of your movements and behaviour, you are also under arrest for a rape in May 1992 in Eltham and a series of sexual offences back to 1989." He again repeated the caution and asked Napper if he understood. Napper again gave a short "Yes" in reply.

Alan said, "We are now going to search you for evidence of offences for which you have been arrested and for articles which may cause harm or injury to yourself or us. As Napper was dressed only in his boxer shorts and was handcuffed the search lasted only seconds. Napper stood forlornly in the centre of the tiny bedsit, bearing not the least resemblance to the monster who had set a murder team hunting him down for the past six months. He looked frantically about him as if expecting help.

Alan said, "Please remain calm, nobody is going to hurt you."

Peter Canavan bent down and, as Napper had his arms pinned behind his back in handcuffs, put Napper's shoes on his feet. Over his shoulders he placed the yellow jacket so often seen by the surveillance team.

Napper visibly relaxed. Alan engaged him in conversation asking which parts of the building he had access to. Napper replied matter of factly, "This room and I use the kitchen and bathroom as well."

Alan asked if he had access to any vehicle or other cupboards or sheds. Napper looked up, resembling a scolded schoolboy more than a psychopathic killer.

"No."

Alan asked, "Where are your keys?" Napper weakly raised an elbow and nodded towards the door from which hung a bunch of keys. "Only those."

The room was very small. It had no windows and the only entry was via the door they had all entered by. It was tidy, everything was stowed away and folded. Alan said to Napper. "Stay calm, the officers will conduct a search. Meanwhile get some clothes on. You will be taken to Bexleyheath Police Station to be questioned." Napper pointed towards clothes at the foot of his mattress and after being released from handcuffs started to get dressed. He dressed in the clothes readily available, dark green jogging bottoms which he overlaid with black trousers. A dark blue T-shirt and then replaced his long, hooded, yellow anorak. No training shoes were in evidence. Alan called in on his radio.

"One arrest, Robert Napper. We are in his room. Can you please send the van to pick him up at the front of the house."

The radio crackled back. "Yes, will do, will notify you when the van arrives. It's on standby and will be with you shortly."

The radio crackled again.

"Do not enter the house, do not search."

Alan recognised the voice as that of DI Pearse.

The officers in the room looked at each other. Alan spoke into the radio. "We are in the house, one arrest, over." The voice on the radio suddenly got louder. "Get out of the venue, the search is illegal ... Repeat do not go into the house." He thought, "Well if this is illegal, I've been getting it wrong over the last 15 years."

He let the radio remain silent for a moment. Then spoke. "Plumstead Control, Any news on the van?"

The radio blared back, "Do not conduct a search." Alan reached down and turned the volume to off. He turned to Napper who seemed oblivious to it. "You will be taken to Bexleyheath Police Station where you will be offered free legal advice. You will be interviewed with a solicitor if you require one. The interview will be tape-recorded and you will be given a copy. Do you understand?"

Napper looked at Alan with an expression almost of gratitude. "Yes."

"In the meantime, as you will not be present when the team searches your flat, can you think of anybody you can trust to be present while they search?" Napper allowed his eyes to wander. "No"

Alan said, "I will arrange somebody suitable." He took Napper into the hallway. The man who had allowed them access still stood on the stairs. Alan looked up. "There will be a search team here in a minute, can I ask you to be here when they search?" The man nodded.

Within a few moments Roger Boydell-Smith appeared in the open front doorway. He glanced at Napper. "It's that one there Rog," Alan said indicating Napper's room. Napper was handcuffed again, this time between Alan and Peter, one to each arm. The three of them walked the short distance around the corner to where the van was waiting. Up until this point, Napper had only spoken in response to questions. As they approached the rear of the van he suddenly looked at Alan and in a staccato voice said, "I heard of the murders in the paper. I don't know Samantha Bisset, I have never been where you said."

Alan released his side of the handcuffs and Peter got into the back of the van with Napper. The female police officer who was the second member of the van crew joined him in the back. Alan jumped into the front seat next to the driver. He took out his incident report book and started writing on the way to Bexleyheath. The unsolicited comment made by Napper could prove vitally important. The only substantive evidence was fingerprints and Napper had just denied he had ever been to the flat at 1a Heathfield Terrace. Alan needed to write it down immediately.

The outer door to Napper's bedsit where he was arrested.
His windowless room was just inside the main door on the left.

CHAPTER 16

At the Police Station — It Can Only Get Worse

The van entered the yard at Bexleyheath Polce Station as Alan was completing his notes. He jumped out of the side door and ran around to open its back door. Napper sat calmly inside handcuffed to Peter Canavan. Alan assisted them both down the steps of the van. The station was newly built to a modern design and well-suited for the arrival of prisoners in vehicles. A short walk brought them into the back of the police station and directly into the custody area. The custody sergeant had been forewarned of their arrival and directed them to take a seat on the bench at the rear of the custody room. Napper was released from his handcuffs and with Alan approached the custody officer cocooned behind his chest-high solid desk.

The formalities began. Alan introduced himself and then Napper. He gave a summary of the arrest and the reason for Napper's detention. The custody officer noted Napper had been handcuffed and then asked him to empty his pockets and place the items on the desk. He raised his arms indicating he had nothing. Alan then searched him finding nothing. The custody sergeant continued with his standard procedures and authorised his detention at 10.06 hours. He was reading Napper his rights when Alan noticed out of the corner of his eye, walking into the charge room, DI Pearse together with a woman he didn't recognise. Pearse approached the desk and without acknowledging Alan spoke to the custody officer. "I am DI Pearse, I am investigating this man on suspicion of a series of rapes. The lady present is a clinical psychologist from the Maudsley Hospital. She will act as an appropriate adult. Napper has had mental issues in his past."

There is inevitably potential for a clash of rank and responsibility in a fast moving situation and Alan had been unaware an appropriate adult had been pre-arranged. The custody officer was unfazed and replied, "I will note the custody record, sir, we are now booking him in." Alan felt prickly but unsure. But sure in his own mind, he wondered why this was happening. The custody officer continued. Whatever the offence, the ritual was always the same.

"Are there any marks or bruises after the use of the cuffs or any other injuries?" Alan pulled back the anorak sleeves and turned Napper's hands over.

"No Sarge."

Alan read through his notes including the comment made by Napper after his arrest about never having been to 1a Heathfield Terrace. The custody sergeant asked Napper whether he agreed with the account of his arrest. He replied, "Yes" and signed the custody record as being a true account.

As the booking-in was being completed, DI Pearse leaned forward and said to the custody officer, "There is fingerprint evidence."

Alan couldn't believe what he had just heard.

He took a step back from the table and faced Pearse.

"Why have you mentioned fingerprint evidence?" scarcely able to keep his temper from boiling over.

DI Pearse was momentarily taken aback.

"We must under PACE disclose it."

Alan was furious. His voice rose slightly.

"No, we do not. Not at this stage. It is for the interview."

Pearse smiled, seemingly sure of his own ground. "I can assure you we must reveal as soon as possible we have fingerprint evidence."

Alan saw red. He hissed, "I can assure you, you c... that you do not. Now please step back from my investigation."

Pearse's jaw dropped as the custody sergeant looked on impartially, then continued with his booking-in procedure after which Alan walked with Napper the short distance to the cells and placed him in one. Napper immediately sat sheepishly on the bench and Alan closed the door firmly behind him and dropped the observation grill. He walked through the charge room and took the stairs two at a time up to the CID office from where he telephoned Bryan Reeve.

"Hello Al, all okay."

"Yes guv. He's booked in, made an unsolicited comment about never having set foot in 1a Heathfield which he has signed as being correct."

Bryan sounded chirpy.

"The search is going well, some good stuff being recovered."

"Guv, I had better tell you, I've just sworn at Mr Pearse and we've had a difference of opinion."

There was a moment's silence, then laughter.

"Don't worry about it Al these things happen."

Alan thought, "Not to me they don't". Bryan continued, "Just get him booked in and arrange for him to give blood. I can't come down there at the moment. Just keep it civil."

Alan went back to the custody suite. Pearse was still there, deep in conversation with Miss Rutter. He thought about apologising, but just then the woman police officer who had been on duty in the police van at the time of Napper's arrest walked through from the cell area. Alan had a thought.

"I just want to ask you. You have been with Napper and close up for 20 minutes or so."

"Yes," she looked up suspiciously. "Why?"

"I just wanted to ask, "How tall do you think he is?"

She pondered for a moment and replied. "About 5' 10"."

"Are you sure?"

"Yeah, pretty sure."

Alan went out into the yard for a breather. The estimate of the woman officer could account for a lot. His police record showed Napper as 6' 1".

The day dragged on, the search continued at its own pace at 135 Plumstead High Street. The FME examined Napper and, with his consent, took a blood sample which was dispatched immediately for analysis. Whilst going through the formalities Alan tried to judge Napper, get a feel for what made him tick. Napper remained silent but co-operative, he stood when asked, he made no requests and when he did speak it was in answer to the most mundane of questions.

Napper was slim and tall, when measured he was indeed 6' 1" but held himself with a pronounced stoop, as if shying away from his true height. He was clean shaven with acne on his face, the acne was more pronounced on his back. He had short dark brown hair, parted to the left and slightly receding at the temples, although not dirty it had a greasy, unkempt appearance.

"Would you like a cup of tea?"

"No. Thank you very much." That same peculiar staccato form of speech. Alan remembered the scene at Heathfield Terrace. Could this quiet, mild-mannered individual be responsible for such an atrocity? Well, only the evidence would show for sure but Alan sensed there was something wrong. Something Napper was concealing from the world, maybe even from himself.

A team meeting was scheduled for 5 pm at Plumstead. All who could attend would be there. Roger and the exhibits team were still combing through the tiny bedsit and would be involved there for a while longer, but information was filtering back of some interesting finds. Items that seemed to confirm Napper was responsible for the murder. The next step was to arrange the interview of Napper.

Banks already had a long list of questions he wanted to put. Bryan Reeve and Peter Canavan were told to prepare the interview. DI John Pearse and Detective Sergeant Eddie Lever were to take over when the murder interviews were complete and interview him with regard to the rape series. Pearse and Lever had intimate knowledge of this series and Banks wanted to keep the two investigations separate. The Green Chain Walk rapes had the potential to turn toxic and he didn't want any fallout polluting the murder investigation.

The meeting was certainly no exercise in self-congratulation. There was an enormous amount of work still to be conducted. The arrest and the subsequent search would generate hundreds of actions. Alan gave a summary of the arrest and detention at Bexleyheath. He made no mention of the radio interruption at the time or his "falling-out" with John Pearse at the custody suite in Bexleyheath, nor was it mentioned by anyone else.

It was explained that the reason Napper had detoured from his usual daily routine was because the day before his arrest he had been sacked from his place of work after several warnings. No direct approach had been made to his employers whilst he was under surveillance and therefore no-one on the police side knew that Napper wouldn't be going into work in the morning. An extraordinary run of lucky incidents had benefited Napper to the last.

The plan of investigation now was to research all of Napper's associates, all of his family and all of his work places back to the year he left Abbeywood Secondary School. A trawl and examination was to be made specifically of Plumstead Police Station records for any other offences he may have committed. Also, starting from the local area and moving outwards, the review of any other similar unsolved cases. Banks was convinced, as were most of the team, that by it's very nature this could not be a one off offence. Especially if Napper proved to be the Green Chain Walk rapist. Five of the rape and sexual assault victims had provided an identical DNA-profile of the offender. With a blood sample now secured from Napper it was only a matter of time before confirmation, or not, would be given.

The team worked late into the night preparing the interview of Napper which was scheduled for the next morning in the new video recording interview room at Bexleyheath. Banks informed Paul Britton of the impending interview and he agreed to attend. Britton was still engaged on another much more high profile murder in West London, that of Rachel Nickell. He was building a reputation as one of the top criminal psychologists in the UK. The profile of the unknown offender provided by him for the BBC *Crimewatch* programme was taken down and dusted off. The gist of it was:

The suspect had in all probability been the victim of violence in his childhood.

He would be the product of a disturbed family life.

He feels undervalued.

He is not a sadist but gained some satisfaction from his interaction with the victim's body.

He may use contact magazines.

He is of normal intelligence.

He will be single and quite able to hold down a low-skilled job.

He clearly has some kind of psychological malfunction which prevents him sustaining any meaningful relationship.

He is not a man seeking notoriety or fame. In fact the opposite.

He will have a history of offences against women and probably cruelty to animals.

He is a watcher and stalker.

Banks had previously shared the profile with the team but hadn't given it overwhelming weight, with the exception of one important detail. Paul Britton had predicted that the person responsible had an overwhelming urge to attack women. This could manifest itself in minor assaults but, given the opportunity, he would feel the need to kill again. No wonder we all had sleepless nights before the culprit was identified. It was akin to manning a defensive position waiting for an inevitable attack.

Re-reading the profile after identifying Napper showed just how close Paul Britton came, it was a very good resumé.

CHAPTER 17

The Interviews

Next day the weather was again kind allowing a clear run down to Bexleyheath for an early start. A small office had been put aside next to the interview room to gather notes and thoughts. The interview room itself was an unknown quantity and nobody present had used one of its type before. Much more spacious than what all were used to. Someone was on hand to explain how the system worked. It had been decided overnight to link the interviewers via earpieces to Micky Banks and Paul Britton who would be monitoring them from another room. Paul Britton emphasised he would only be there to guide the questioner by watching the reactions of Napper during the interview.

Alan went down to the custody suite to introduce himself to Napper's solicitors and to fetch Napper up from the cells. There was no sign of yesterday's appropriate adult, Miss Rutter. Instead there were Napper's solicitor Mr Herman together with an appropriate adult provided by Social Services, a Mr Simms. After booking Napper out of his cell and introducing him to the two men Alan led the way to the interview room.

DI Bryan Reeve and DC Peter Canavan were the first two interviewers. Bryan made the introduction to the tape and began the interview. Napper gave a "No comment" reply to all questions. Bryan who suffered from poor hearing and was having difficulty telling what was being said over the earpiece, called a halt. He addressed Micky Banks, "Sorry guv. I just can't get to grips with this, I can't hear what's being said over the earpiece and I can't strike up any rapport with him. I think someone else should try." Banks looked-up. Alan was the only other officer in the room. "I prepared the interview with Peter, I'm happy to go in."

Meanwhile John Pearse and Eddie Lever entered the interview room. Pearse conducted the interview on the Green Chain Walk rape sequence and succeeded in some degree in prompting Napper into talking more freely in his stop start style, although Napper made no admissions. The interesting part of Napper's speech was his tendency to use rather long but sometimes inappropriate words which he would inject into his wordplay. An example would be when asked if he was in a particular place he replied, "I was there legitimately, I had no different purpose."

Ten minutes were spent going through the major points again and then the interview recommenced with Alan and Peter Canavan at 11.51 am. Napper was already seated together with his solicitor Mr Herman and the appropriate adult Mr Simms, He looked a little nervous. His hands were clasped in front him and he rubbed his fingers together. His face was expressionless, his pale blue eyes roaming around the room, his rather petulant mouth slightly open revealing protruding, discoloured teeth. Alan dragged his attention from him thinking, "No doubt he is summing me up too, and not being complimentary."

Alan introduced himself although it was clear Napper recognised him. He then explained the recording equipment, Napper nodded perfunctorily. Alan explained that he could stop the interview whenever Napper felt he needed a break. Napper looked towards his solicitor, not at Alan.

There are many techniques to be employed for interview, all are relevant to the circumstances and the character of the person being interviewed. Alan decided not to constantly refer to pre-planned notes but rather to create the atmosphere of a chat. To engage the person opposite, and above all to let them speak. Never to interrupt them once in flow, even if it was not the way the interview was expected to go. The opening, after the mandatory caution was to explain why he was being interviewed and how the interview was for his benefit as much as for anyone else's.

"Do you understand Rob?"

"Yes, I understand fully."

Alan attempted to tempt a response from him by asking straight questions which had no obvious bearing on the offence.

"How long have you lived at 135 Plumstead High Street?"

Napper looked at his solicitor and replied, "I wish to make no comment at this particular moment in time."

Invoking his peculiar staccato speech pattern, not surly, not defensive, quietly this continued. Alan tried a change of tack and referred more directly to the murder scene. This at least elicited a response. After two or three unanswered questions, Napper started to swallow and become agitated. His prominent Adam's apple moved rapidly in his throat. He suddenly blurted out, "This is heavy." He looked to his solicitor and said, "I want to stop the interview thank you very much and consult with my solicitor." Mr Herman stepped in and asked for a consultation and the interview was suspended.

After a few minutes Napper felt able to resume although the same pattern was repeated, always ending as soon as any questions about the murder were raised. Alan kept hearing Paul Britton's voice in his earpiece, excitedly asking him to ask this question and that. But Alan knew that just asking the proposed question would not be sufficient and Napper would not reply. The interrupted pattern happened several times with Napper turning to his solicitor at the slightest excuse to ask for an adjournment. This occurred five times with the longest time Napper was able to continue only 27 minutes.

Alan decided to stop the interview but not before telling Napper the list of evidence against him. Napper continued sitting back, but in obvious discomfort, his pale eyes now fixed on Alan as if willing him to disappear. He told Napper that police were still researching further evidence and as soon as this became available he would interview him again. He then left the interview room with Peter Canavan. In essence the interview had been a failure. Looking back, Alan realised he had not prepared properly, he had been surprised by the willingness of Napper to respond to questioning, just so long as it did not refer to the murders. Far more probing was required to establish more of a rapport and to show or at least feign an interest in Napper's delusions. He had failed to change tack and think on his feet. The opportunity to interview Napper again never arose.

DI John Pearse conducted the interview into the rape series and was far more successful in getting Napper to talk. This was no doubt thanks to his studies for a doctorate in Criminal Psychology, which was well under way by that time. Although he did manage to elicit more responses, Napper doggedly continued to deny any involvement in any of the rapes. Under the rules of PACE suspects can only be kept in police custody for a limited time before they must either be charged or released. This is initially a period of 24 hours. Extensions can be applied for, initially through a chief officer of police and then through a magistrate. The extensions had been used-up and charging would have to follow. Once somebody has been charged the opportunity is very limited to re-interview them.

Alan felt deflated as he talked over the interview with Micky Banks, Bryan Reeve, Peter Canavan and Paul Britton. Banks tried to put a decent spin on it, "Don't worry about it Al. It's plain he's bonkers."

Alan suddenly realised he had a phone call to make and hurried off to a quiet office. Jack Morrison answered.

"Hello Jack. How's Margaret?"

"She's not so good. Having a bit of sedation."

"Sorry to hear that Jack. Give her my regards. Have you heard the news? We arrested someone for Sam and Jazmine's murder yesterday."

"It wasn't on the news up here but I had someone from a newspaper knocking on my door this morning. He told me there had been an arrest." There was a long pause.

"Do you think he did it Alan?"

"Yes Jack. We are pretty sure. I've just been interviewing him."

"Did Samantha know him?"

"No Jack, it looks like she was stalked."

A moment while that thought settled.

"Aye. It's not good"

"Listen Jack, I'll send someone round from the local police. They can assist should you get pestered with callers. In the meantime, refer any press to the Press Bureau at Scotland Yard."

"Thanks Alan. We don't want to talk to anyone at the moment. Least of all the press."

"It's best Jack, please call me any time you need anything."

Alan gave Jack his bleeper number then did something against all regulations and passed his home telephone number.

"Thanks Alan. Take care and come up and see us when you can."

"I will Jack."

The investigating team had now moved back to ramshackle Thamesmead where work on the new lines of enquiry was continuing apace. The search of Napper's bedsit had revealed another *A to Z* similarly marked as the first one seized from his Reidhaven Road address in 1993 when he attempted to obtain MPS identification passes. Within the pages, clearly marked was a reference to Samantha's address at 1a Heathfield Terrace.

An officer from the Operation Eccleston team, DC Christine Smith was allocated the task of studying both Napper's *A to Zs* and producing plans from which conclusions as to the whereabouts of other offences and hiding places might be deduced. Also in the flat were piles of loose sheets of paper covered with doodles, sketches and random words. The words were of a disturbing nature and referred to unarmed combat, knife attacks and alternative words for death amongst many other seemingly obscure references. These were all handed to Christine for her to try and make sense of.

Disappointingly no training shoes of any description were found in the bedsit but what was found was the shoe box for a size 9 Adidas training shoe together with a receipt for their purchase prior to the murder. The shoe was of a type identical to the one from which a composite shoeprint had been found at the murder scene.

There was a small quantity of literature in the flat. Some of it referred to pornography in the form of low quality "girlie" magazines. There were magazines also on combat and adverts for hunting type knives. Photocopied pages of a book called *The Dragon's Touch* referred in detail, including graphic pictures, to how to incapacitate another person and deliver death blows. Particular attention was made to the neck area. There was also paperwork showing that Napper had purchased hunting knives. He received one by registered post on the 13th July 1992 described as a "Special Operations Government" knife costing £62.45 pence. In December of 1992 he received another knife. Described as a SOG Recon for the same price.

A heavily used *Collins Dictionary* was found which contained many underlinings of words. Nearly all the marked words had a death or sexual connotation to them. A Sanyo music centre was found to have concealed a coiled length of synthetic rope in the battery compartment together with a pass to "Enskilda". This proved to be a car park pass issued in 1993 by Enskilda Merchant bankers, London EC4.

In a corner of the room was a khaki coloured haversack which upon examination contained nothing but pebbles. In the only cupboard, on the floor, was a red metal toolbox. Inside the lid was appended a printed note.

"LONESOME? BORED? LIKE EXCITEMENT?
WANT TO BE NOTICED? WANT TO MEET STRANGE NEW PEOPLE?
THEN JUST LEAVE YOUR SECURITY CONTAINER OPEN."

The box contained two hunting knives with eight inch blades but these were not the ones described in the receipts. Roger carefully peeled back the home made warning notice on the box. There was nothing written on the obverse but there was a clear outline of a shoeprint. It was of an Adidas Phantom Low trainer. The composite shoeprint formed a crucial part of the evidence. From receipts at Napper's bed-sit it was shown that on or about the 12th January 1993 Napper had bought a pair of Adidas Phantom Low training shoes size 9 from M & M Sports. The shoes are described as white with three black Adidas stripes on the side with other grey markings.

Napper paid by cheque, £67.48p dated 12th January 1993. On or about the 25th of the same month the order was sent to Napper at his then address of 63 Reidhaven Road, Plumstead. The shoe box recovered from the flat at 135 Plumstead High St was identical to the box which had been despatched by M & M. Sports. The shoeprint of an Adidas Phantom Low trainer was exactly the same as the composite shoeprint obtained from Samantha's flat.

Contact had been made with Napper's mother who still lived locally. Pauline Napper was in shock, she knew her son Robert had had mental illness problems from an early age. She told a tragic story of Napper's allegedly abusive father and also about how a friend of a relative had taken Napper on a camping trip when he was about 12-years-of-age. Pauline had thought this would encourage Robert to open up. Instead the "friend" sexually-assaulted the young Napper. A a middle-aged man who had befriended Napper's mother was subsequently convicted of the sexual assaults at the Central Criminal Court.

Napper had always been a "loner" and difficult to engage socially, she had never known him to have a girlfriend. The last time she had seen her son was on Christmas day 1989 five years previously. They had parted on good terms. According to Pauline Napper in 1989 Napper had approached her in a state of distress. He had taken an overdose and confessed to his mother he had raped a woman. Pauline felt that he was attention seeking but nonetheless went to Plumstead Police Station to report the matter. She only had sketchy details and times. The officer behind the desk made enquiries in the CID office and then spoke to Pauline. He told her that there had been no offences reported which matched the description Pauline had given.

In fact a particularly nasty rape of a young mother in her own home had been committed at around that time, that of Julia Henly (not her real name) in Purrett Road which had gardens backing onto Winns Common. The suspect had gained access to her house in the morning through an insecure back door. He had walked calmly past children having their breakfast and raped their mother upstairs in one of the bedrooms. Afterwards he just as calmly walked out the way he had come. This offence would prove to be the first known assault committed by Napper in his series of Green Chain Walk rapes. DNA evidence had been obtained from the victim.

The offence in Purrett Road appeared to be marked in Napper's first *A to Z*. A copse of Birch trees is clearly marked which look down onto the victim's address. This high point also looks over the common northwards to Heathfield Terrace. Extensive enquiries were made at Plumstead to find any record of Pauline's visit about suspecting her son of rape. No record was ever found and the officer on duty could not be identified. However there is little doubt that Pauline was telling the truth.

Answers were pouring into the incident room but just as quickly more questions were arising. The office at Thamesmead was buzzing. There could be little doubt now that the Bisset team had got their man. Banks directed Alan to attend Bexleyheath the following morning and charge Napper with the murders of Samantha and Jazmine. The time was running out for detention. One extension had already been granted but time is always short and the last thing needed was to be forced into a position where the suspect would have to be released.

Alan tidied up his reports as darkness eventually fell. The weather had been sunny and the long May days were stretching-out. The setting sun could be seen between the grey tower blocks. Alan thought to himself, "How many people are out there enjoying a golden evening?" The office was thinning out as he got up to go. He looked up at the large white board containing lists of outstanding actions. At the top of the board were the names of the victims, next to that had now been added the name of Robert Napper. Three people unknown to each until that fantastical, obscene attack in the November before.

Something caught his eye. The dates of birth. Both jotted in marker pen in short hand. Samantha 25/02/1967. His eyes fixed next on the word Napper, next to it; dob 25/02/1967. This was an amazing coincidence. He thought back to Samantha's last telephone call on the night she was attacked, to her Pisces star line, the one she often called. Alan stared at the board. He had just arrested and interviewed a seemingly mentally challenged individual who had taken the lives of two innocent people, one of them a child. Napper it seemed had had an unbelievable run of luck not to have been captured before this. But the thing that rankled with him mostly was the birthday, the 25th of February. It was Alan's too.

CHAPTER 18

The Charge

O n Sunday Alan made his way back to Bexleyheath Police Station. There was still no reply from forensic services on the results of the DNA check on the blood sample submitted. The charge room was quiet and the custody sergeant was able to give Alan his full attention.

Alan went through to Napper's cell. Firstly looking through the wicket he saw him seated on the cell bunk, staring vacantly at the wall. Upon opening the cell door Napper looked at him, pale blue eyes unflinching and weak mouth set in a petty scowl. Alan spoke first. "Morning Rob. You will be charged with the murders of Samantha and Jazmine Bisset. If you would follow me." Napper rose slowly to his feet. Alan thought to himself, "I should hate this man." But the feeling of hatred would not materialise, instead he felt a strange sensation of pity. For a moment the images of Samantha and Jazmine left him.

Alan waited for Napper to exit the cell and pointed down the short corridor towards the custody desk. Nobody else was in the charge room. The melee of the day before had completely subsided. The custody sergeant had already typed-up the charges and as Napper stood before the charge desk he read them out. After the obligatory caution, Napper made no reply. The sergeant informed him he would be detained in custody until appearing before the magistrates and then added he would be photographed and have his fingerprints taken.

The photograph room was adjacent to the custody office and Alan and Napper went in. Alan said, "Just wash your hands in the sink over there." Napper carried out the instruction, still without speaking. As he pulled down the roller towel Alan said, "Make sure you dry them properly." A quick glance from Napper and he again complied.

"Now, sit down there." Alan indicated a chair which was fixed in front of a white wall. Alan pulled over a box of letters and filled in Napper's name and custody number on the board in front of him. He walked to the camera.

"Look straight ahead."

Napper's eyes fixed on the camera and Alan clicked the shutter.

"Beautiful, we'll make sure your mum gets a copy."

No reaction.

Alan laid out the brass fingerboard, dabbed six or seven blobs on it from a tube of fingerprint ink, picked up the roller and rolled the blobs out to an even, sticky expanse on the board. When he was satisfied the ink covering was even, he told Napper to stand.

Napper sidled over to his side. Alan felt his presence, he stood 6' 1" and Napper was at least as tall, his close proximity did not feel threatening. Alan took Napper's right hand in both of his. "Just relax and let me do the work." He rolled the index finger onto the inked board. The hand felt weak, slightly clammy, not labourer's hands, on the small side. Alan continued until all the digits, palms and chops (the side of the hand running back from the little finger) were copied onto the fingerprint form.

"Now wash your hands again."

Napper looked as if he was about to say something, but didn't. He followed Alan over to the where the old-fashioned height measuring equipment was fastened to the wall. "Stand with your back to the wall and stand up straight."

Alan carefully dropped the horizontal bar to the top of Napper's head.

"6' 1". Then he walked Napper over to the custody sergeant. "All done Sarge." The sergeant looked up from his computer terminal. He looked towards Napper.

"Do you require anything?"

Napper at last spoke. "No ... Thank you very much."

Alan took him back to his cell and quietly closed the door. He opened the wicket and watched Napper resume his seat on the bunk and his stare at the wall.

Alan made his way back to the Thamesmead incident room to report back to Bryan. The office was still busy with officers writing up actions and progressing the massive amount of work generated by the arrest.

Roger had finished at the scene of Napper's flat. He looked as relaxed as always. "Well Al, looks like we've got our man, there's a lot of incriminating stuff in his bed-sit. Who knows what the *A to Z* will tell us. Christine is starting to put together a chart of all the markings and doodlings."

Alan sat back with a cup of tea. "Yeah, it's going to be interesting looking at those. He's a strange bloke Roger. You wouldn't think he would say "boo" to a goose, now we've got to make sure we really build a case against him. Any news on the DNA?"

"Not yet," he smiled, "what do reckon the betting is?" Alan laughed. "They must be sweating, but it's a foregone conclusion I reckon." Roger gave the carousel a gentle spin. "No doubt in my mind."

An office meeting was set for 6 pm. Micky Banks stood in front of the action board puffing at his roll-up while Bryan Reeve called the office to order. Banks, looking more relaxed than he had in months, addressed the meeting.

"You all know by now Napper has been charged with murdering Samantha and Jazmine. Until we get a DNA result we don't know if he was responsible for the rapes. In the meantime Operation Eccleston is setting up ID parades to see if any of the victims can pick him out. We are lucky insofar as the press haven't yet shown a huge interest but I expect that to change when and if Napper is identified for the rapes. When that happens I expect you all to keep what goes on in this enquiry within these walls. There is an enormous amount of work still to be done and we are not going to lose this job after having come so far. The team will remain full strength until further notice. Operation Eccleston will remain a separate enquiry but obviously close links will be maintained."

He stopped. The room was in silence.

"We will now revisit any other crime scenes for which he may have been responsible. It appears he hasn't travelled much and seems to stay local, but keep an open mind." Another pause. Somewhere outside a bird was singing, it must have been well and truly lost.

"Right. Get on with it then."

A sudden bustle as papers were gathered and phones were reached for. Alan headed for the door. There were a couple of hours of the weekend left and he was going home to enjoy it. Tomorrow would be another early start for the first appearance at the magistrates' court. It could be gauged then just how much the press were interested in the story.

CHAPTER 19

The Progression of Increased Violence

To be able to properly investigate the murders of Samantha and Jazmine it was necessary to research the sequence of Green Chain Walk rapes. At first glance the string of offences bore the classic hallmarks of a psychopath who grew ever more cunning, yet reckless, but more importantly ever more violent. Studies of this type of offender clearly show they learn as they progress in their offending. Even so, nobody could have predicted the spree of violent attacks against women on open park land would result in the murder of a young woman and her child in their own home.

Almost predictably, Robert Napper had a troubled childhood, from an early age there were concerns about his mental health. However, he wasn't found guilty of his first criminal offence until he was 20 in 1986 when, in August of that year, he was convicted at Bexley Magistrates' Court of carrying a loaded air weapon in a public place. He had been stopped by police in the company of another youth in New Road, Belvedere (a sub-district of Bexley) and when caught he tried to conceal the weapon before being searched. He pleaded guilty and was given a conditional discharge for one year.

In 1989 he was living locally in the family address at Mannister Road, Abbey Wood and was unemployed at the time. On 10th August that year a young mother resided at Purrett Road, Plumstead, SE18, with her two young children aged eight and five years. Purrett Road runs down into Plumstead from Winns Common, the back gardens of the houses in Purrett Road back onto the common. Purrett Road is only one mile approximately from Napper's then address of Mannister Road.

Subsequent examination of the first of the *A to Z*s of Napper to come into police possession in 1992 reveal a point on Winns Common marked by three distinctive birch trees. This is a vantage point, not only over the rear of Purrett Road but also across to the northern side where Heathfield Terrace (the home of Samantha and Jazmine) is situated and that Napper was to visit a little over four years after the Purrett Road incident to such devastating effect.

The rear garden of the house was separated from the common by a chain link fence. The fence was in a state of poor repair and allowed easy access to the garden. On the day in question, Julia Henly had opened her kitchen door into the garden to allow the cat in at 7 am. She prepared breakfast for the children and they sat down to eat it while she went upstairs to her bedroom.

At 8.30 am Julia looked-up to see a man standing in the bedroom doorway. He was unknown to her and she described him as white, 5' 10" tall, of medium build with mousy hair and aged about 19 (Napper was 23 at the time). He was wearing cheap looking faded jeans and a brown bomber jacket. He took out of the right pocket of his jacket a Stanley knife. The bottom half of his face was covered with a patterned, beige coloured cloth. He ordered her onto the bed and then pulled her T-shirt up and over her head where it was tied with a piece of flex across her eyes. Julia was terrified, especially for her children. The intruder asked her name which she gave and then he raped her, ejaculating inside her. Before leaving he undid the tie and told her to stand in the corner and count to 20. As he left he said, "Do you want a bit of advice? Don't leave your back door open."

Shocking as the attack was, no further violence was used. The attacker went downstairs and walked past the children, who were still innocently eating their breakfast, into the rear garden. Julia went to the rear bedroom and saw him exit via the insecure fence onto the common. She then lost sight of him as she called for the police.

This attack bears many similarities to the Bisset murders. Both had obviously resulted after some form of surveillance. Both victims sunbathed in their gardens; the victim at Purrett Road in her bikini, Samantha topless. Both positions of sunbathing were susceptible for a voyeur to watch them from covered woodland. Shortly after this offence, on 6th September 1989, Napper took an overdose of a mixture of paracetamol, aspirin and other drugs and was admitted to the Brook Hospital.

He returned to the family home the next day and a week later moved out. It was when visiting his mother in late October/early November one month later that he confessed to her that he had raped a woman on "Plumstead Common". This prompted her to make enquiries at Plumstead Police Station only to be told erroneously that no such incident had occurred. She put it down to Robert's mental state and the manifestation of his increasing fantasies.

It should be made clear that Plumstead Common and Winns Common adjoin and are commonly known locally as Plumstead Common. Checks carried out after this information had come to light, subsequent to the Bisset murders, showed that the rape in Purrett Road had been properly recorded and was shown as adjoining Winns Common. This simple confusion led to the tragic error which may have put a stop to the subsequent string of violent offences against young women.

Samples were taken from the victim and sent for DNA analysis. A positive result was given but it did not match any known person in the criminal index. This was in the very early days of taking DNA samples and at the forensic laboratory a mistake was made with a part of the sample. This mistake meant that it could not be relied upon as evidence. Four years later the victim could not positively pick out Napper in the identity parade following his arrest for the murders of Samantha and Jazmine.

Time marched on and it appeared that the Purrett Road rape had been a one-off. Then on 10th March 1992 another attack was made on a young woman. This time on the Cordwell Estate SE13 which is about two miles distant from where Napper was living at the time at 189 Well Hall Road. The victim was on her way to visit a friend, when at 8.45 pm in Cordwell Road, as she approached an alleyway leading from Northbrook Road onto the Cordwell Estate, she noticed a man behind her. He was walking in the same direction as her on the opposite side of the road ten yards behind her. Being early March the sun had set and it was quite dark. She turned into the alleyway and when she had covered three quarters of its length she heard the sound of footsteps behind her.

Starting to feel concerned she looked over her shoulder and saw the same man only five yards behind her.

She exited the alleyway and crossed a small courtyard towards another alleyway, as she did so the same man ran towards garages on her right. She was seriously alarmed as she entered the second alleyway and she started increasing her pace. As she hurried along she was suddenly grabbed from behind by her right arm. The same man confronted her. In his right hand he was holding a knife which he pointed towards and close to her stomach. He spoke in an aggressive tone. "If you want to live don't make any noise."

He dragged her back to the garages and pinned her against a wall. He tried to kiss her mouth and told her to undo her jacket; upon her refusal he forced her clothing up and grabbed viciously at her breasts. At the slightest sign of any resistance he laid the knife against her stomach and said, "Shut up. If you want to live, be quiet."

Without warning he punched her hard three or four times on her left cheek. Her head smashed against the garage wall. He pulled her jeans and knickers down and pushed her to the ground, kicking her legs apart. He lowered his own jeans and attempted to rape her but failed to penetrate her. Suddenly, as if distracted, he looked to one side and stood up. He started to kick her in the head as she attempted to protect herself with her hands and after six or seven blows he walked-off back down the alleyway. The victim stumbled to her feet and staggered the short distance to her friend's house where the alarm was raised. When examined by the police medical officer Dr Clare Roden she was found to have a cut mouth; the left side of her mouth and jaw were severely bruised and swollen. Dr Roden's view was that she had been the victim of a very violent assault. Samples were taken from the victim and her clothing was sent to the police laboratory for examination.

The attacker was described as a white male aged about 20 years. He was 5' 8" tall and of stocky build, he had dark brown straight hair. The victim went into greater detail. She said he had brown eyes and a clean complexion without spots. She was able to tell from the short amount of speech he had made that he had a south east London accent. He was wearing a black bomber-style jacket and blue jeans. From analysis from a seminal deposit taken from her jeans a profile was produced of which there was less than one chance in 1.3 million that a person chosen at random from the Caucasian population would have a similar one. The profile matched the (albeit corrupted) profile of the victim from Purrett Road. Although the police did not know it at this time, the profiles both matched Robert Napper.

Within eight days on the 18th March 1992 the rapist struck again. The site of the next attack was in Vista Field off King John's Walk, Eltham SE9. King John's Walk forms part of the Green Chain Walk and is surprising rural in its aspect. The walk drifts through open fields where horses graze and patches of woodland dominate to the south of Eltham Palace. At about 8 pm in the evening the victim was walking south along King John's Walk. It was dark and at this section of the lane there is no street lighting. She heard steps behind her, turned and saw a man walking towards her. She put her head down to avoid eye contact and as the man passed her she felt uncomfortable. She stopped and decided to walk back the way she had come. She stopped again and looking back saw the man far away in the distance. At this point she made a fateful decision to detour across Vista Field (so called as it offers a view of London in the distance) and walk westward over the field to her parents' house. It was a shortcut but at that time of the evening, dark and isolated. She hadn't gone far when the man who had passed her earlier suddenly confronted her. He was holding a knife with a 6" blade in his right hand. He was wearing a balaclava but the face part was open, only covering his head. He used odd expressions of speech,

"Get down on your knees, I've got this. I'll use it." "I'm not going to hurt you, I'm not going to screw you. I just want to put my tongue in your mouth, I want to kiss you." He forced her backward and kneeled between her legs. He pushed the knife hard up against her left breast before pulling it away and lifting her upper clothing and bra. He lay on top of her and started to kiss and suck her breasts. He then asked her to "go down" on him, to which she feigned ignorance.

Several times he blurted out, "Shut up, or I'll knock you out." At the same time threatening her with his clenched fist, he stripped her of her lower clothing and attempted to rape her but could not manage an erection. He said, "This will go in. I will do it."

The terrifying ordeal continued without full penetration. When he eventually stopped, he rose to a kneeling position and placed the large knife between her legs with the point towards her vagina. He said. "You could have got this." He moved the knife up and down her body between her breasts and chin in a horrible simulation of what he would actually later act out for real on Samantha Bisset. He got to his feet and walked-off, back towards King John's Walk. The victim dressed and ran down across the field where she dashed into a shop from where police were called.

The attacker was described as, white about 5' 7" tall, slim, collar length mousey coloured hair aged about 19 years. When he had spoken, he had a strange inflection in his voice, as though he were in an interview. He pronounced his words very carefully. When examined, the victim was found to have a wound in her left breast. It had been caused by a knife, a small puncture half an inch wide and a quarter of an inch deep. A DNA profile was raised from seminal fluid staining on the victim's clothing. It matched that taken from the other two offences.

It was now established that there was a dangerous assailant operating in south east London who was targeting young women in violent sexually-motivated attacks. A team was set up at Eltham Police Station with a remit to find the attacker. The enquiry was given the title Operation Eccleston and led by Det Supt Steve Landeryou. The team had one great positive piece of evidence. They had a profile of the DNA of the attacker. However, at this time, DNA was not regularly taken from people coming into police custody and the science of DNA had only recently been used as an effective evidential tool. There was a lot of resistance to its use by sections of the public who believed it to be an invasion of privacy in the extreme. There were powerful factions of the judiciary who seemed to want to destroy its credibility through the courts.

The sequence of vile attacks continued relentlessly. The next attack would bear alarming similarities to the murder of Rachel Nickell who was to become Napper's most infamous victim in September later that same year. Again in King John's Walk, Eltham on 24th May 1992, two months after the last attack, another victim was walking the tranquil way between Eltham towards Mottingham at 2 pm. She was pushing a buggy which contained her two-year-old daughter. Ahead of her in the distance she saw the figure of a man cross the path from her right to the left. Unconcerned she continued along the pathway until she passed the spot where the figure had disappeared. She suddenly noticed he had re-appeared behind her. She heard his footsteps as he gained on her. As she turned to look she felt something pass over her head. Suddenly she realised that the object over her head was a ligature and it was being tightened around her neck. She instinctively let go of the buggy and grabbed at the thick cord. A voice ordered her to put her hands behind her back and the cord was relaxed.

She pleaded, "Please leave me, because of my little girl" and was roughly told to "Shut up." She found herself on her back. Later examination showed she had been subjected to considerable force including blows to the head and body. She felt dazed. The man roughly tried to remove her top but she resisted. He pulled down her shorts and panties and as in previous attacks could not complete the full sex act because his penis could not achieve a full erection. Suddenly he stood up, pulled-up his shorts and Y-fronts and ran off northwards towards Eltham.

The victim managed to stagger with her child to Middle Park Avenue where she collapsed at the door of her mother-in-law's house. She was so covered in blood that her mother-in-law did not at first recognise her. Whilst waiting for the police to arrive the victim told her mother in law that the attacker was "really tall." She also told a police constable, PC Fleming at the hospital, when asked by him "How tall was he? Was he as tall as me? I'm 6' 3" tall", "Yeah, about your height." Unfortunately when describing her attacker later she amended the height estimate to only 5' 7". Why this was done has never been clearly established.

The victim suffered severe bruising to her head and upper body. The injury to the area of the right eye orbit resulted in loss of vision and required laser treatment. In her statement she described her attacker as, white, 5' 7", slim with short brown hair aged between 26 and 30 years. He had dirty grey teeth and a spotty chin. He was wearing a T-shirt, blue shorts and light grey socks, she had no recall on what type of footwear he had on. A DNA profile was obtained from semen left at the scene and this again matched the profile of the previous attacks.

It may never be known if there were any other attacks which may have happened but gone unreported. All similar attacks in that area and in the wider sphere of the Metropolitan District and Kent were looked at by the Eccleston investigating team. It seemed only a matter of time before he would strike again. The investigators hoped against hope they would identify him either by the patrols they had set up or by the net they had cast to obtain DNA samples from likely suspects. They believed it was only a matter of time before the offender fell into their trap. The sequence of offences had achieved a high profile with widespread press interest. They had a detective inspector on the team who was forceful and driven, he was studying for a doctorate and was open to modern ideas in the profiling of offenders. His name was John Pearse.

In an effort to widen the scope of the enquiry the expertise of a psychological profiler were sought. The team thought themselves lucky to secure the assistance of the man who was riding a wave of success in this new field, a consultant clinical psychologist whose name was Paul Britton. Britton, after consultation and many meetings with the leaders of Operation Eccleston, produced a profile of the man they were looking for:

He would be aged between 18 and 25 years and unlikely to over 28.

Of low to average intelligence who will not have performed well academically.

If employed it will be undemanding intellectually.

His work may be in a group but he will shun women colleagues.

Any female friends will be much younger, less threatening, more easily impressed.

He is a reckless risk taker, who whilst offending is relatively unconcerned about apprehension.

He derives satisfaction from the fear he produces in his victims.

It is clear from offence style that interaction with certain victim responses could lead to the death of a victim.

He expresses considerable rage and anger. There are indications he is taunting the police.

He is likely to be known to police covering the areas of the assaults.

He may be a burglar.

He has connections to the area by residence, schooling and employment.

He may have moved away between the first and second offences.

He will be expected to suffer from the following:
1. Sexual deviant fantasy.
2. Sexual dysfunction; erectile problems, primary premature ejaculation.
3. Inability to sustain heterosexual relationships.

He may have a background of less serious offending; i.e. indecent exposure or voyeurism.

The victims could be regarded as having similar signs of "vulnerability" although little by way of physical similarity.

He will bring himself to attention in one of three ways:
1. By information provided by the public or area police officers.
2. Being caught during an offence.
3. By elimination process based upon an examination of records.

If arrested it is important to consider the use of an appropriate adult in interview.

He is dangerous and will continue to offend and may escalate his violence according to victim reaction.

Finally, in summary, the profile suggests a full re-examination of the first indoor rape scene together with a visit to all surrounding householders and neighbours.

This profile was to prove prophetic and incredibly accurate. After the positive identification of Napper through DNA was established, identity parades were set up for the rape and sexual attack victims to see if they could identify him. Julia Henly the rape victim from Purrett Road did not pick out Napper in an identification parade held on 4th July 1994 (four years after the offence).

SC the rape victim from the Cordwell Estate had no difficulty in picking-out Napper on the parade, she was 100 per cent certain. The DNA profile matched Napper and gave a less than 1.3 million to one chance that a male Caucasian chosen randomly would have a similar profile. LM who was attacked in Vista Field identified Napper in an identity parade as the man who had attacked her. The DNA comparison confirmed that the semen found at the scene came from Robert Napper. CM attacked in King John's Walk whilst with her two-year-old daughter also picked-out Napper at an identification parade. The DNA profile comparison with a sample from the scene and Napper proved positive with a less than one in eight million chance of it belonging to anyone else.

There was no lingering doubt that Napper was responsible for the Green Chain Walk rape series despite his persistent denials. Attention could now be concentrated on the Bisset murders.

CHAPTER 20

Other Incidents

The murder team now had full access to the rape enquiry files. Reading through them, many unanswered questions began to fall into place, especially after the search of Napper's address at 135 Plumstead High Street and the recovery of his second *A to Z* road map book. The first *A to Z* from his arrest in 1992 was found still to be in the property store at Plumstead. There were clear markings in both the of these, seized in 1992 and 1994, which indicated the area of King John's Walk, Eltham, where the last three rape offences took place. Also recovered from Napper's Plumstead flat was a hand drawn map which marked Winns Common and the circle of birch trees which overlook both the Common and Purrett Road where the first rape happened inside a house.

Lists are the curse of an investigation, but must be thoroughly completed. They will include lists of actions and messages, and of possible suspects (however unlikely). Lists of witnesses who may have seen a yellow van which resembled the one seen outside Samantha's address. Lists of telephone numbers dialled by Samantha whose corresponding identity needed to be established. Lists of men who had answered her adverts in dating sections of newspapers and magazines. To prioritise is essential, but, nothing can be overlooked.

Another early start and the office at Thamesmead was in a buzz. The result of Napper's blood test had returned from the laboratory. The DNA recovered from all four rapes matched his. Now there was no doubt. The enquiry now widened to search still further afield for other possible offences. Between the time of his arrest on 25th May 1994 and the date of the last known rape on 24th May 1992 two years had passed. Given the short time span between the rape offences and the Bisset murders, what had Napper been up to in between?

The rape enquiry offered up one incident which happened on 19th August 1992. At the time Napper was still living at 189 Well Hall Road, Eltham and working at Serco in the old Royal Arsenal, Woolwich. Shortly after 6 pm on a calm summer's evening on the 19th August 1992, a young woman walked from the Queen Elizabeth Hospital across Woolwich Common to a bus stop in Academy Road. She waited at the bus stop to catch a bus south towards Eltham. She was the only person at the stop when a man appeared. She later described him as white, about 5' 9" tall, slim build with short medium brown hair, parted on the left side. He was aged about 25 to 30 years. His complexion she described as grubby and he had a pock-marked, long face and staring eyes set off with a pair of "sad looking lips". He was wearing a bright red T-shirt and blue jeans cut off below the knee.

He spoke to her using a south London accent through bad, uneven, dirty teeth. His speech was curiously pronounced in a careful way. He asked her if he could go up Academy Road and asked in such a way as if to suggest the road was military property. She replied to him that the road was clear, and he walked off in the direction of Eltham. After about ten minutes the man returned to where she still waited for the bus.

He said, "You can't walk up the hill."

When asked, "Why not?" he said, "there are dead bodies up there. Someone has been dragged to their death."

She started to worry about the man's behaviour, especially as he drew ever closer to her. A bus drew up and, despite the fact it wasn't the one she was waiting for, she jumped on it. At first the man stayed on the footpath, but, at the last moment before the doors shut he jumped onto the bus. She felt very uncomfortable as the man continued to stare at her. As the bus passed Shooters Hill Police Station she got off, the man also got off using the front entry door. Now feeling really concerned she walked quickly towards the police station. Upon seeing this, the man suddenly ran off across Eltham Common, disappearing into the woods behind the Welcome Inn public House in Well Hall Road.

She did not see the man again but shortly after the incident she spotted a Photofit in a local newspaper created by one of the rape victims and was so struck by the likeness to the strange man she had encountered near Woolwich Common that she contacted the police and confirmed she believed the man in the Photofit and the man who had approached her were one and the same. Where the woman had last seen him behind the Welcome Inn was immediately opposite where Napper was then residing.

Much closer inspection was given to the series of rapes using the *A to Z*s and other maps and doodlings of Napper as a cross-reference. Closer scrutiny was also given as to why the Operation Eccleston rape enquiry had been run down given the violence of the attacks. It is an unfortunate truism in any enquiry which does not produce a suspect that pressure will inevitably mount to shut it down. After the spree of attacks in 1992 no further incidents were reported. This may have been because of the publicity given to the public, especially young women, to beware the presence of a serial attacker. It may have been the attacker had been arrested on an entirely unrelated matter or moved elsewhere. The fact for the enquiry team was that there were no further offences. This was a success story for the safety of young women on the Green Chain Walk but a severe curtailment of any possibility of any suspect coming to light. Inevitably the enquiry was cut back until a point was reached when a decision had to be made whether resources could be justified in continuing.

An enquiry cannot just be abandoned mid-stream. All possible leads must be shown to have been followed and satisfactorily eliminated. As the operation had reached the threshold of a major enquiry it had a computer account on HOLMES (Home Office Large Major Enquiry System) and would be almost instantly ready, should further offences be committed or a suspect come to light, to be instantly re-opened. Pressure was mounting on Landeryou to close the enquiry and free his investigators for ever more pressing, current investigations.

The first three victims of sexual assault had described the assailant as around 5' 8" tall. The fourth victim amended her first report of the attacker being tall to being 5' 7". How such a discrepancy could have happened may never be known. In any event a policy decision was made to accelerate the shut down of Operation Eccleston. To facilitate this it was decided to eliminate any suspect who was less than 5' 5" tall and more than 6' 0". This decision was to have catastrophic results.

As the investigation started to wind down, information came into the incident room from two different sources both naming Robert Napper as being a good likeness for the well-publicised Photofit. One of the calls was from a work colleague of Napper at Serco (at the MOD at Woolwich). He contacted the Eccleston incident room with information on his misgivings about Napper. He described him as a "paranoid schizophrenic" and informed the rape investigators that Napper bore a good resemblance to the Photofit.

In a later statement, after Napper's arrest for murder, he expanded on his knowledge of Napper stating how women at work were frightened of him and referred to him as "The Creep". Napper's antagonistic attitude towards women was confirmed by the female work staff. Napper was at this time, August 1992, living at 189 Well Hall Road. His next door neighbour also contacted the enquiry team stating that Napper bore a resemblance to the Photofit. He had seen it in the *News Shopper* newspaper. Not only did he bear a resemblance but he would see Napper going out alone late at night, he had also heard from one of the lodgers at the same address as Napper that he had had his bags packed for weeks. As a result of this information two detectives were despatched to see Napper and assess him as a suspect. Upon speaking to him on 28th August 1992 they found him co-operative, quiet, unflustered. They also found him to be 6' 1" tall. They asked him to attend Eltham Police Station to provide a blood sample. Napper readily agreed and a date was set for the 2nd September 1992.

No rapes had been known to have been committed since the 24th May but the request was made within ten days of the woman being frightened by the man at the bus stop on Woolwich Common. The male who was behaving in a disconcerting manner towards the female witness was last seen running into woods behind the Welcome Inn public house. This public house (now a housing block) was situated almost opposite 189 Well Hall Road where Napper was residing at the time of this incident and also when the request for a blood sample from him was made. Napper failed to appear on the date agreed. On the next day the detective who had asked Napper to attend Eltham Police Station handed a sealed letter to one of his colleagues to deliver to Napper. It informed Napper to attend Eltham Police Station for a blood sample to be taken at 7.30 pm on 8th September. This was the next available appointment. The letter was delivered at 189 Well Hall Road on the 4th September. Napper again did not keep the appointment.

This was obviously a reason for some concern; however, it should also be borne in mind that refusals of requests from police to submit to a blood test in criminal enquiries are not as unusual as the law-abiding might think. People will refuse on many grounds. The request to Napper to provide a sample was, as it said, a request. To treat failure to attend as grounds for suspicion is certainly an issue and has been hotly fought over in the courts over the years. In this case, supervising officers assessed the refusal, looked at the height of the suspect and made the decision to rule out Napper as a suspect on the grounds of the policy decision they had made to eliminate all men over 6' 0" tall.

Operation Eccleston continued to wind down and no further action was raised to re-visit Napper. He was eliminated from the enquiry.

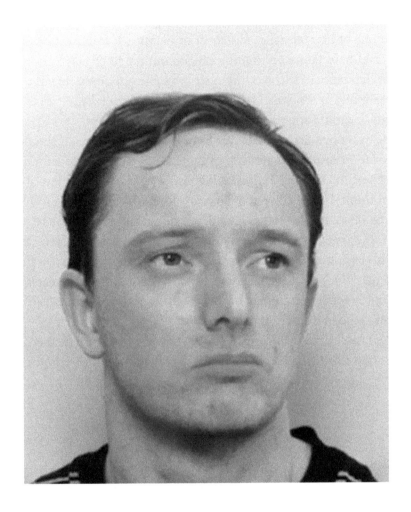

Robert Clive Napper.

CHAPTER 21

Causes for Concern

Roger Boydell-Smith was sorting through all the exhibits taken from Napper's Plumstead High Street address. The two *A to Z*s were of particular interest. The first was seized after Napper's arrest on firearm offences on 27th October 1992. Contained within the book, was a Greenwich Borough gym card. This referred to a fitness club in Elm Terrace, Eltham, one at which for a brief period Napper had been a member. The card, however, belonged to a woman whose address was given as Grangehill Road, Eltham, a short distance from where Napper was living in Well Hall Road. The card was tucked into the page which contained the address of Grangehill Road. Roger showed the card and the book to Alan.

"This looks interesting Al. The person on the card is a relative of the guvnor, Bryan. He wants you to go round and see her and take a statement." There was a photograph on the card. A pretty woman in her early twenties, fresh faced, aged about 23, with shoulder length fair hair. The description was the same as all the victims of rape, the young woman frightened at the Woolwich bus stop and most significantly of all Samantha Bisset.

Roger opened the *A to Z*. "Look at this." On the page containing Grangehill Road was an inked circle around the name Grangehill next to the house of the young woman on the gym fitness card. Alan retrieved and read the interview of Napper which he had given after his arrest when found in possession of the *A to Z*. Napper had been much more talkative when interviewed under caution for the firearms offences. The interviewing officers felt there was something more, but were unable to put their finger on it. When asked where he got the card from he replied, "I found it outside 189 Well Hall Road."

He expanded, falling over himself to be helpful. "I found the pass outside a house. At the time I'd only just come walking in from my work. My intention was I shall place it in the relevant page of the *A to Z* and give it back to her." He paused with one of his peculiar mannerisms and continued in his haltingly strange vocabulary. "But obviously had it waylaid." The interviewing officer said, "It was in the page marked Grangehill Road. Is that correct?" Napper agreed it was.

Alan telephoned the victim and made an appointment to see her that day. The door was answered by a man who introduced himself as her father-in-law. Alan was shown through to an immaculately kept living-room and offered a cup of tea. He was introduced to the young woman in question, an attractive, fair-haired woman whose fitness card photograph did not do her justice. Alan was struck how similar she was in appearance and height to Samantha Bisset.

She had joined the fitness club in June of 1992 and at about the same time had started a new job as a barmaid in the Welcome Inn, a public house referred to before and opposite the address where Napper was living in August 1990 before departing suddenly on 24th September 1992 after the police request for him to provide a blood sample, when he moved to Reidhaven Road, Plumstead. In September 1992 her purse had been stolen from the staff changing room at the pub. Access to the changing room being at the back of the kitchens was difficult for any members of the public to reach. Within the purse was the Eltham fitness card.

Apart from possession there is no evidence to suggest Napper as the thief, however, having come by the fitness card, if he were concerned, he could have returned it to the address which was printed on the rear of the card which stated clearly, 'If found please return to the Waterfront Leisure Centre, Woolwich' which was on his way to work at Serco. Or, he could have returned it to the Eltham Fitness Centre, an address he was familiar with. Or, he could have walked the few hundred yards from his then address to Grangehill Road and posted it through the door. He did none of these things and was still in possession of the card a month later, having marked the young woman's address in his *A to Z*.

The young woman had never met Napper and had no idea who he was. A lucky escape, particularly bearing in mind that a high profile murder on Wimbledon Common, which was eventually to be linked to him had happened on 15th September 1992, at about the same time as the card was stolen. After the Eltham fitness card incident there were no more reported offences which could be definitely attributed to the Green Chain Walk rapist.

Alan was called in to see Micky Banks. "We've got a lot now on the Napper family and his background but we still haven't contacted the father. Napper's mother says he emigrated to Australia and hasn't heard from him since. Find him and inform him what has happened." Alan thought for a moment. "He is supposed to have been violent towards all of the family, are we going to assist if he wants to come back to the UK?" Banks smiled. He was far more relaxed since the arrest of Napper. "Just find him and suss him out."

After a few enquiries Alan established that Brian Napper had emigrated to Australia in 1976. Through Australia House he was found to be living at an address in New South Wales. After talking to the local police in New South Wales and without giving any information away Alan arranged to telephone Brian Napper at a convenient time on his home telephone number. The telephone call abroad had to be arranged through the switchboard at New Scotland Yard. After the call had been organized, at 10 am on 19th July 1994 Alan sat at his desk in the Thamesmead office and took a deep breath. The phone was answered by a man who spoke with an Australian accent. Alan said, "Is that Mr Brian Napper?"

"Yes it is."

"Mr Napper, my name is Detective Sergeant Jackaman. I am calling you from the Metropolitan Police in London."

"Alright. What's it about?"

"Firstly I need to establish I am speaking to the right person. Are you Brian Napper and do you have a son called Robert?"

There was a pause. "Yes, what's he done?"

Alan felt it was a little odd to ask what he had done rather than "What's happened?"

He pressed on, "For clarification could you tell me his date of birth?"

"Haven't got a clue."

"The year perhaps?"

"Um, lets see. Around '66 I think."

Alan felt he had to bring the matter to a head.

"I have some rather shocking news for you, are you sitting down? Is someone with you?"

"Just tell me."

"Your son Robert has been arrested for rape and murder and is in custody here in London. He has been charged."

There was a much longer pause, several seconds.

Then in a raised voice Brian Napper said, "I blame his mother."

Alan was a little taken aback by this reaction.

"Now is not the time to apportion blame, Mr Napper," all the while thinking, "This is the man who allegedly beat his wife and thought nothing of putting fear into his small children."

"Mr Napper, I will give you the telephone number of the police station here." He read out the number whilst Napper wrote it down, then repeated his name.

"Call that number any time if you have any questions, alternatively you can go through the local police. Now, you have had a big shock. Think about what I have said. I will call you the same time tomorrow."

Again a long pause.

Alan said, "Is there anything else you can think of right now that I can help you with?"

"No."

"Okay then Mr Napper I will call you again on this number the same time tomorrow."

The phone went dead.

Alan replaced the receiver and made a cup of tea.

The following morning Alan went through the same routine. This time the phone at the other end rang... and rang. Nobody picked it up. Neither Alan nor the enquiry team heard from Brian Napper again.

CHAPTER 22

What Else Had Napper Done?

There was no doubt in anyone's mind on the Bisset murder team that there were other offences which had been committed by Napper to be uncovered. It didn't make sense to believe otherwise given the frequency and increased violence of the rapes from March 1992 through to the middle of that year, culminating in his strange behaviour with the girl on the bus at Woolwich in August 1992 and the incident with the fitness card belonging to the young woman living in Grangehill Road, Eltham that September. Then for no apparent reason this behaviour stopped. It was established by now that Napper continued throughout this period to reside in the Plumstead area. The team looked more closely at his behavioural patterns.

Later interviews with his neighbours and those who had worked with him were carried out. There were reports of Napper often being seen talking to himself and also shouting at the sky. Several witnesses voiced their concerns of his aggressive attitude towards women in general and women in positions of authority in particular. Then there was the discovery of markings in his two *A to Zs*. These directed the eye towards places where he was now known to have attacked women and included obvious markings around the area of Winns Common and Samantha Bisset's flat. The maps and other doodles came under closer scrutiny and attempts were made to try and decipher some of the arcane wording contained within them.

Surveillance had shown Napper's interest in knives and guns, this reinforced by receipts found in his flat which recorded the purchase of several hunting knives which had been manufactured with the express purpose of causing injury and death and sold with little camouflage to their intent and use.

Napper had purchased by mail order a magazine devoted entirely to the sale of hunting knives. He also bought by mail order two knives, one called a KHM18 Mirage combat knife and another a KS100 knife and scissors sharpener; payment was made by cheque and the items despatched to 189 Well Hall Road to Mr R Napper. There was also the book *The Dragons Touch* which referred to "weaknesses of the human anatomy." These knives were in addition to the two SOG hunting knives also sent by registered delivery to that address for Napper on 13th August 1992. This was one month before the murder of Rachel Nickell on Wimbledon Common. None of these knives had been recovered which added substance to the theory of a "hidden stash".

Actions were raised to research the many questions raised. Priority was given to the possibility of Napper having a stash somewhere, where he could keep his trophies, such as the missing part of Samantha's body, other keepsakes and the knives. Searches were conducted, led by Roger in all of Napper's old residences including lofts and gardens. At the search at 189 Well Hall Road, Roger found in the loft a tent and a gun/knife magazine addressed to Napper.

Alan was tasked with searching the routes marked along the Green Chain Walk and areas of common land where Napper may have hidden his hoard. Some areas were easily pinpointed from marks in the *A to Z*. In other hand drawn maps identification was far more difficult to decipher and they contained many strange symbols and words. Somebody had the bright idea of contacting the Army at Woolwich barracks to ask for their assistance. This was when the skill of "Winthroping" was first mentioned. Winthrop was an Army officer who devised a way of searching in Northern Ireland during the troubles in the 1970s and 1980s. The basis of it was that pre-planned attacks on Army patrols would necessitate hiding heavy weapons beforehand to be readily available when needed. Thinking this through, Winthrop realised the weaponry would need to be hidden in a place which could be readily identified by the terrorists. It might be a solitary oak tree, a break in an old wall or anything which could be described to the persons carrying out the attack and easy for a terrorist to find.

Transferring this logic, it followed first identify a place which has the potential as a good spot to make an attack and then scan the horizon and surrounding area for a likely place to be easily identified by the intended terrorist to find his equipment. This method had achieved some spectacular successes when applied in Northern Ireland. Captain Bacon of the Royal Artillery at Woolwich and a couple of his men were happy to oblige and helped Alan's small team comb likely places selected from the information available throughout Napper's known hunting ground.

Whilst this was going on another historical incident came to light which showed the theory of the hidden stash to be more than just a theory. A search of the collator's records at Plumstead again revealed a curious incident which, at the time, seemed unimportant but in the light of the murder investigation grew in significance.

In the early part of 1992 a report of criminal damage was made by a young blond woman who lived alone in a ground floor flat off Plumstead Common. Within the report it was recorded that she had the impression of seeing someone in woodland opposite to where she resided. One evening, after dark, she was shocked when one of her windows was suddenly broken. At first she couldn't find out what had caused it. Then she found a spent bullet embedded in the wall close to where she had been standing when the window was smashed. She called police and a scenes of crime officer examined the scene. He retained the spent bullet. The crime was never solved and was recorded at Plumstead Police Station where it entered the crime book as a criminal damage. No similar incidents were recorded.

On 19th February 1993 two boys were playing in the woods at Winns Common. In the undergrowth, buried in a shallow hole, they found a large biscuit tin. The tin was marked "Happy Shopper Assorted Biscuits". Upon opening the it they found within it, carefully wrapped in cloth, a Mauser .22 handgun, serial number A02837. Wisely the two boys immediately informed their parents who in turn informed the police. The biscuit tin was recovered and the Mauser pistol sent to the police firearms laboratory to be tested for fingerprints and to cross check it against any criminal offences where shots were fired. These both proved negative.

Roger, whose task it was to trawl the crime book at Plumstead and other police stations spotted the entry of criminal damage to the window. It could so easily have been overlooked, but Roger, ever the thorough investigator, saw beyond the initial entry and dug deeper. The scenes of crime officer who had attended the criminal damage to the window was found. It transpired he had not submitted the spent bullet and had, unaccountably, not realising its significance, kept it. It lay undisturbed on his mantelpiece at home.

Roger also found a reference to the biscuit tin containing the Mauser pistol. He submitted the spent bullet to the firearms laboratory to be compared against the Mauser pistol. It was confirmed as a match. It was a proven fact that the bullet had been fired from the .22 Mauser found hidden in the woods at Winns Common. Roger then recovered the biscuit tin which was still in the property store at Plumstead and submitted it for a fingerprint examination. On the inside of the lid was the palm and fingerprint of Robert Napper. This was all too late of course and didn't help in the murder or rape cases as there was no intimation of the use of a firearm in any of these attacks, but it certainly added impetus to the stash idea. The exact spot where the biscuit tin had been buried was marked in Napper's *A to Z*.

At some stage Napper had purchased the Mauser, had identified a young woman victim and for reasons known only to him fired through her window. He had then kept the firearm concealed in a biscuit tin buried on Winns Common where he could easily retrieve it. Roger visited the scene from where the shot had been fired. The young lady's window was clearly visible from woodland on the common. In the hours of darkness it would have been an easy shot. Roger was convinced having viewed the spot both in daylight and in darkness that the shot had been directly aimed at the proposed young woman but the shooter had been deviated in his aim by the shadow cast by a standard lamp.

DC Christine Smith from the Operation Eccleston enquiry was making progress on Napper's doodles and markings in both *A to Z*s and systematically went through them all. From this she produced A3 maps where the doodles were superimposed over the markings. There were hundreds of doodles, many making no obvious sense, or single odd words but intense study started to reveal patterns which coincided with the *A to Z*s. From the jumble started to appear clarity. It was pioneering work, an amazing effort and, even after many years, when looked upon, still a thing of wonder.

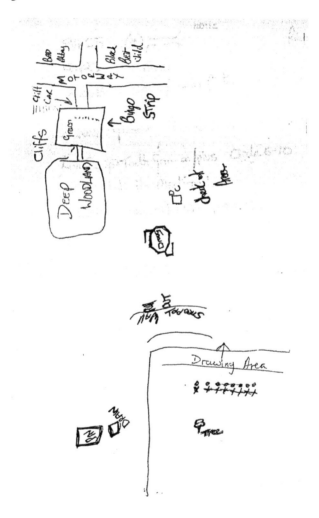

Examples of Napper's doodles.

145

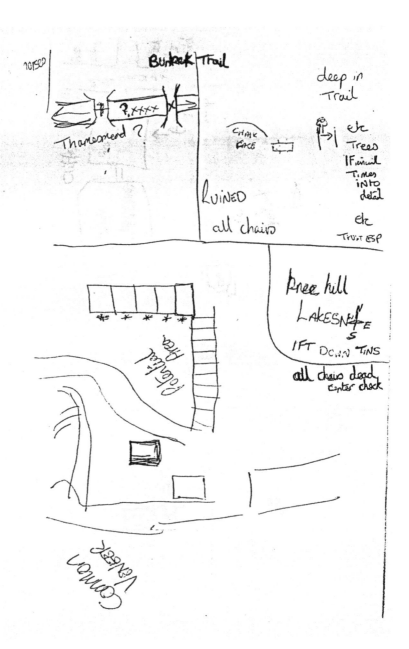

CHAPTER 23

Preparation for Trial

For many years within the MPS there has been an attitude at senior level that once a person is charged with an offence then it must necessarily follow that resources will no longer be required to bring the matter to court. The higher the level of command the more tenuous the grasp on the fact that, in serious cases such as murder, after charge is the crucial part of the investigation and support must be given to allow as full a case as is possible to be presented to the court. This entrenched attitude was to be highlighted to the detriment of the service in the Damilola Taylor enquiry.[1] Improvements were made after the Taylor Review but old bad practices have a tendency to creep back.

Recognition of the importance of the Bisset case had at last happened and one of the top lawyers at the CPS was appointed to handle the case, Mr McCann. Subsequently a very experienced barrister was appointed for the prosecution, Nigel Sweeney QC, who had as his junior another very experienced prosecutor David Spens. The defence appointed as their barrister William Clegg QC a man renowned for presenting the most comprehensive defences in support of his clients. Clegg was currently defending another man suspected of murder. His name was Colin Stagg. Stagg had been charged with the murder of Rachel Nickell and since 18th August 1993 had been remanded in custody awaiting trial.

---

1. Damilola Taylor was a ten-year-old schoolboy who was murdered on a south London housing estate in November 2000. In April 2002 the trial of four local youths concluded without any convictions. The police handling of the investigation came under criticism and a review was conducted. One of the criticisms levelled at the police concerned the post-charge phase of the investigation and the associated work necessary in preparing the case for trial was less than well-managed. This resulted in a recommendation for future investigations that any need for a post-charge strategy should be identified and agreed in major cases as a matter of good practice. (*Damilola Taylor Murder Investigation Review.: Report of the Oversight Panel*, 2002).

The early part of committal proceedings for Napper was fairly straight-forward and it caused no surprise when he was remanded in custody pending trial on a date to be arranged at the Central Criminal Court, the Old Bailey. Conferences were arranged between counsel and key members of the murder team. Although Napper had also been charged with two rapes and two attempted rapes relating to the Green Chain Walk Operation Eccleston enquiry, the two enquiries remained separate.

Back at Thamesmead all outstanding actions were listed for completion. Now a confirmed suspect had been identified, some actions could be written off. Some new actions were still being raised as the enquiry tidied-up and prepared for the forthcoming trial. Just before the arrest of Napper in May 1994 the office manager Detective Sergeant Bob Thomas had retired. His place as office manager had been taken over on 22nd April by WPC Mary Salt. Mary had been working on the team as an indexer since the day after the murder. She was well-respected within the office although the appointment was highly unusual. The role of office manager on a murder enquiry was always the preserve of an experienced detective sergeant. It was perhaps felt that as the enquiry was already up and running it would not be worthwhile to appoint another detective sergeant to replace Thomas. When he retired, the identity of Napper had yet to be established and, from an overview, it still appeared to be an unsolvable murder of two "unimportant" people from an unfashionable outer London borough which did not require the services of a valuable detective sergeant. The appointment however was inspired. Mary revelled in the role, after Napper was arrested she continued as office manager.

Nigel Sweeney and David Spens at least recognised the importance of the investigation, and more importantly saw the pitfalls ahead when coming to trial. The plea was not guilty on all counts. Almost immediately after Napper was charged, and despite D S Banks best efforts, the enquiry team was cut back. Within one month of being charged the murder team was reduced still further until there were only five full-time members left. By the end of May 1994 the incident room at Thamesmead was required for other uses and the small team remaining could not justify the space. They were moved lock stock and barrel to Belvedere where they set up in a two room office on the top floor. Belvedere is an old-style police station on the outskirts of London, built in a time when police stations were a centre point of their community. Nominally self sufficient with a charge room, four cells and a front office open to the public, the station was now a satellite of the modern Bexleyheath Police Station. Detective Inspector Bryan Reeve remained in nominal command but in August 1994 was seconded to another enquiry. Alan remained as acting Detective Sergeant with Roger retaining the vital job of exhibits officer. Only Detective Constable Peter Canavan remained as the outside enquiry officer. WPC Mary Salt continued as office manager assisted by Enid Lamb as indexer. Enid had also been on the enquiry from the beginning, she was an experienced, popular lady with a quick and ready wit. She had been returned to the central murder pool along with the other indexers in May but, within one month after lobbying by Bryan Reeve, was returned to the murder team. The only other member of the team left was Police Constable Rick Davey. Rick remained on loan with the team from Plumstead and was invaluable for his knowledge of analytical data and his computer skills. As the rump of the Bisset team forged onwards, at the Old Bailey in September 1994 the trial of Colin Stagg collapsed in sensational circumstances.

The enquiry room at Belvedere matched the décor of the rest of the building; old wooden desks with spindle backed chairs, the walls festooned with white boards soon to be filled with action lists and other aide memoirs of the enquiry. A HOLMES connection wasn't needed as the enquiry was still being run from the now overloaded and creaking carousel which had been carefully dismantled and re-assembled for the move. The team were joined by the rump of the rape enquiry, Operation Eccleston, in the shape of DI John Pearse, Det Sgt Eddie Lever and WDC Christine Smith.

Operation Bisset took up the larger part of the office, Operation Eccleston the smaller section. The best part of the arrangement was that Christine and Rick could work together on the *A to Z*s, sketch maps and other doodles in comparative peace. They were to produce some amazing and, for the time, cutting-edge work in graphics for eventual presentation at court. A frequent visitor to the small office was junior prosecution counsel, David Spens. He generally arrived late in the evening from other work at court and would produce sheaves of requests for the team to resolve. He would do this in such an affable and friendly manner that it wasn't until after his departure from the office that Alan and Mary realised how many actions had to be raised to cover the demands. The greatest enemy of all was time. The news reached the office that the date of the trial was to be in September 1995. As it approached the meetings at the Temple with Sweeney increased in time and intensity. Bryan was heavily involved in writing the final report, a mammoth task, which needed to include the rape offences, as by now the indictments had been joined. Back in the tiny office the task sometimes seemed insurmountable. The only thing to do was to plug on and answer the requests and demands of counsel.

Christine was gradually making sense of the *A to Z*s, she produced charts showing where the marks were compared with known offences. Most of these marks were around the area of south east London encompassing Plumstead, Woolwich, Eltham, Lewisham and Bexleyheath. The small team pondered over the charts; they became all consuming, there were still many mysteries yet to be solved in the sprawling coded messages. One particular marking drew the attention of all. Christine had recorded this as mark No. 76. The vast concentration of markings, over 80 in all, were centred around the areas of the Bisset murders and the Green Chain Walk rapes in a fairly confined area. However, there were others. There were six clear marks north of the River Thames, three in Hackney, two in Barnet and one near Regents Park. These required further research for any other possible offences.

The only other markings from both *A to Z*s were both in West London. One in Hayes and the other, a clear rectangle, marked out Isabella Plantation which forms a part of Richmond Park. All research of Napper could give no clue as to why Isabella Plantation was so highlighted. He had no known connection there. All other markings predominated around where he was born, lived and worked. It seemed so random. One morning Roger called Alan over. "Take a look at the Richmond Park marking again Al." Alan looked hard at it.

Roger continued, "This was in the first *A to Z* which was seized in October 1992 when Napper was caught trying to impersonate a police officer." Alan continued to stare at the mark. Roger said, "The Rachel Nickell murder was on the 9th September, one month before this *A to Z* was seized." Alan nodded. Roger pointed at the map, "See how close Isabella Plantation is to Wimbledon Common." Alan looked up. "Yes. We know that already and if you remember Micky Banks has already contacted the Nickell team about the Isabella mark and was told they already had a suspect."

Roger shifted in his seat, "Yes I was there Al, but look." He was pointing to a slight mark on the page of the *A to Z*. It was not a mark made by a pen, it was more of a scratch, as if someone had scraped away a tiny portion of the surface of the book. The scrape was on the page referring to Wimbledon Common.

Roger looked up. "Would it surprise you to know that mark is in the exact spot where Rachel Nickell was murdered?" Alan grabbed the book. He reached for a magnifying glass and closely studied the page where he could see a definite mark.

"Jesus Roger, you are onto something here." Alan was on the phone to Bryan before saying anything else.

Bryan's gruff voice answered.

"Guvnor, can you get over here? Roger's found something significant."

Whilst waiting for Bryan to travel from Hither Green to Belvedere, Alan scrutinised the second *A to Z*. The page containing Wimbledon was examined in minute detail. There was no similar scratch or marking in the area of Wimbledon Common.

Bryan arrived and also looked carefully at the markings. "I can see there is something," he said, "but it's very faint. Have it submitted to the lab again for ESDA" (A process for highlighting the faintest of writing on paper, usually used for indented writing on second, third or even more underlying pages). "In the meantime contact the publishers. See if the print copies have the same mark."

Roger and Alan were getting more and more excited about the find and looked again for any other similarities between the rapes, the murders of Samantha and Jazmine and the murder of Rachel Nickell in Wimbledon. One of the most intriguing similarities was the resemblance of a Photofit from Wimbledon Common to Robert Napper. Alan tasked himself with finding out where Napper was on the day of the murder. Rachel was killed on 15th July 1992. At this time Napper was working for Serco and based at the old Woolwich Arsenal. He had worked there from November 1989 until being made redundant on 18th September 1992.

Alan drove down to the old Arsenal in Woolwich where he had an appointment with the site manager. A short tour of the old buildings in which Napper had worked followed. They had been stripped bare, all the forms which Napper had been involved in looking after had been transferred to Llangeneth in Wales. The whole site was a ghost town, it was awaiting a complete transformation into waterfront housing. The site manager was equally unable to help with employment records of the personnel who had worked there until recently; nothing remained on site at Woolwich and he directed Alan to Serco head office in the city of London. A search was made at head office and work records of all staff were found, including those of Napper. Unfortunately the record was brief in the extreme and didn't contain any attendance details.

This was a blow to the enquiry. If Napper was working at Woolwich on the day of Rachel's murder he had an alibi for himself as Wimbledon is at least an hour's journey away. It was for the enquiry team to prove he was *not* working on the day in question, not the other way round. Further enquiries with the Ministry of Defence Police who had responsibility for policing Woolwich Arsenal during the relevant period also failed to shine a light on the movements of Napper at the relevant time.

Contact was re-established with the Nickell murder team. Alan telephoned their office and asked to speak to DCI Wickerson. He had worked with him in the past and most contacts between units are made this way. He was informed Wickerson had moved on after the collapse of the Colin Stagg trial. Eventually Alan spoke to somebody working in the office. He explained how the findings about Napper's connection with the Nickell murder were raising concerns. This was greeted with a frosty response.

With the benefit of hindsight, a veritable chorus of tut-tutting may be heard from the legions of armchair investigators who can now see the obvious. It must be borne in mind that the Nickell enquiry team had a firm initial suspect in the form of Colin Stagg. They had poured time, effort and resources into their investigation. They were under intense public scrutiny via the media. The very last thing they needed was for a rag tag team from the other end of the Metropolis coming-up with an unlikely theory that they had another suspect.

Napper had no known connections to Wimbledon or anywhere in west London. The odd couple of entries in his *A to Z* when compared with the mass concentration of entries in south east London seemed unimportant. Napper was apparently employed on the day of the Nickell murder in his regular place of work in the Woolwich Arsenal. The murder of Rachel bore no obvious similarities to the murder of Samantha and Jazmine Bisset insofar as one was outdoors and the other in the victim's home. Alan told the listener he was awaiting the result from an enquiry with the *A to Z* publisher and the conversation ended.

The publishers of the *A to Z* were contacted. It is a peculiarity of such intensive investigations that the investigator finds out facts which nobody else would ever know or need to know. *A to Z* handbooks are printed in batches. Each batch has its own identifying number which is imprinted on each individual map book. It was therefore a simple task to obtain from the printers a copy of the *A to Z* from the batch which matched the *A to Z* with the apparent mark in Wimbledon Common. A copy was delivered to the office in Belvedere and eager eyes looked on as it was opened at the relevant page. There as plain as day was the same mark in exactly the same place. It was a printing blemish.

This did not deter the team at Belvedere. Other research had been carried out and a feeling was growing that Napper could be responsible for the murder of Rachel Nickell. This hypothesis was not shared by the Nickell team however and it was with a sigh of relief that they greeted the news of the *A to Z* printing blemish. The positive rectangle in Isabella Plantation, Richmond Park was a mile from the murder scene and easier to dismiss. It was a case of 'Don't call us. We'll call you'.

The theory of Napper's involvement with Rachel Nickell was discussed with David Spens on one of his frequent visits. He listened patiently then explained that there were more pressing matters on the Samantha Bisset and rape enquiries. Matters that needed to be addressed with some urgency. The court date was fast approaching and the case was throwing up unforeseen difficulties. There was a genuine fear that a conviction may not happen. This investigation was strapped for manpower and time, the job in hand was the priority. It was again discussed with DI Bryan Reeve, Bryan was enthusiastic but more practically-minded. He looked at the sheet containing the similarities to the two murders and said gruffly, "Maybe Al, but we've got to get this job together first. The Nickell team won't cooperate, they are still sure Stagg is their man. Once we've put this job away we'll look at it again."

Roger and Alan left it at that, but often referred to the strange parallels and the indisputable fact that sexually-motivated killings are so very rare. What are the chances of two psychotic, sexually-motivated killers operating in the Metropolis at the same time? Or even in the same public park, as Paul Britton had pointed out.

A difficulty had been identified in the rape series investigation. The first offence which had been committed inside a house in Purrett Road had produced a problem with the DNA evidence. A mistake had been made at the laboratory whereby one of the samples had become contaminated through an error at the lab. It was policy in the event of such an occurrence that the entire batch would be deemed unreliable. This had the unfortunate result of negating the DNA evidence against Napper for the Purrett Road offence. The victim had been the only one unable to pick out Napper at the subsequent identity parades.

It must be remembered that the application of DNA evidence in 1994 was still very much in its infancy. There was a real concern that, should the prosecution attempt to proceed with the Purrett Road offence with a sullied exhibit, the defence would use the fact of that one example to discredit all the other offences. DNA evidence at this time was being widely attacked in the courts as being unreliable. The Purrett Road offence was the real link with the murder of Samantha and Jazmine as all the other offences had been committed on open ground and, viewed in isolation, had no comparable factors to the Bisset murders. This coupled with the fact there was no DNA evidence at the Bisset scene and there had been a problem with the main stream of evidence, i.e. the fingerprints, caused counsel grave concerns.

The decision was made not to proceed with the Purrett Road case and to firm up the fingerprint evidence at Heathfield Crescent to the last degree. This involved an exercise in continuity to prove that the fingerprints taken at the scene were absolutely incapable of falling to any suggestion that they may have found their way to the points of contact within the flat by any other means than by Napper on the night of the murder. If the fingerprints had been identified immediately this tortuous task would have been unnecessary. Without fingerprint evidence the case against Napper was not a foregone conclusion.

It was also unfortunate that none of the fingerprints were in blood. This could mean they were left there at any time other than at the time of the murder. Napper's statement to Alan, "I don't know Samantha Bisset. I have never been where you said" went some way but could be knocked down or interpreted in other ways. From experience he knew that the best way to present a prosecution was to think defence.

The work continued to pile-up as Mary kept the office moving smoothly forward, raising actions and filing results in the now monstrous carousel. Bryan completed the bulk of the report and Alan was tasked with keeping it updated and adding to it as the trial date closed in.

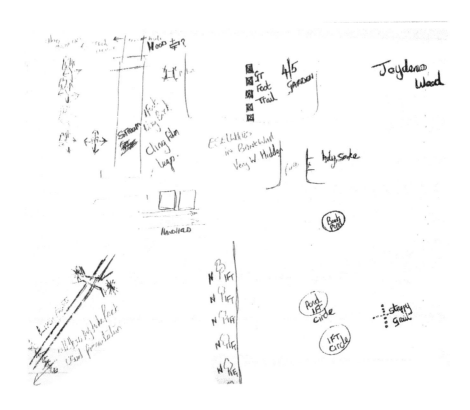

Napper's strange 'doodles' were studied closely by
Christine Smith and the Bisset investigation team as were
the curious markings on his two *London A-Z*s.

CHAPTER 24

Meanwhile in Wimbledon

The team at Belvedere prepared for the forthcoming trial. After a few postponements a trial date was fixed at the Central Criminal Court, 2nd September 1995. The small team after making rudimentary enquiries of possible other offences concentrated on the murder of Samantha Bisset to the exclusion of any other theories. They had to ensure all relevant statements and additional statements were supplied to the CPS and all requests of prosecuting counsel were carried out promptly. As the trial approached the requests increased in volume. The preparation of the case became all-consuming for those involved, to the neglect and detriment of all else. The task of disclosure of evidence alone took weeks of work; a vitally necessary task whereby the investigative work is made known to the defence team.

Before disclosure every document must be scrutinised for sensitive information which is then graded as to its sensitivity. The sensitive disclosure list is submitted to counsel via the CPS for their approval. It is vital that the defence are given access to every document to which they are entitled, failure to do so can mean losing the case in any future hearing. At the time (and alibi apart) the defence could "ambush" the prosecution case at any time by "springing" a new line of defence, but the reverse was impossible (something that has now been made more balanced by disclosure requirements and changes to the right to silence).

Elsewhere, in west London, another enquiry was reaching its zenith. On the morning of 15th July 1992 a young woman, Rachel Nickell was out walking with her young son Alex and her dog in a beauty spot on Wimbledon Common when they were attacked and she was stabbed to death. Despite the fact there were estimated to be over 500 people on the common at the time, the only witness to the attack was Alex, who was yet to reach his third birthday. The murder immediately attracted massive publicity. A young, attractive woman had been stabbed to death in a public place in the presence of her infant son. The offence was horrific, but accompanying factors drove the media into frenzy.

The location near the Windmill on Wimbledon Common was in a generally financially comfortably off district of London. The common is situated adjacent to the A3 which leaves the area of Outer London at this point into Surrey. The crime was committed on a summer's day at about 10.25 in the morning in a park frequented by hundreds of people daily. The only apparent motive for the murder was one of sexual assault, but this had culminated in the victim being stabbed 49 times. Some of the wounds being after death.

At the site of the murder stood a lone silver birch tree. Not particularly significant to anybody at the time, but a curiosity when linked to the significance silver birches displayed in the maps of Robert Napper. The list of injuries was truly horrific and will not be dwelled upon here, suffice it to say they bore a similar pattern to the injuries later suffered by Samantha Bisset, using the same type of weapon.

Police set-up their murder incident room at Wimbledon Police Station under the direction of DCI Mick Wickerson. It quickly became obvious that a massive input of resources would be required. The murder was already attracting a mass of incoming information consequent on press interest, especially attractive was the offer of a £15,000 reward by the now defunct *News of the World* for information which would lead to the arrest of the killer. The information pouring into the information room had to be prioritised and acted upon quickly. No expense was spared. A team of almost 50 detectives and office staff was rapidly assembled. Wimbledon Police Station was not set-up for the installation of the HOLMES computer so management services were tasked to install the necessary wiring. They completed it in record time. The large squad were squeezed into an entirely inadequate space but, as most of the personnel were working outside from the office they managed with a slice of desk sharing.

From day one there were problems with the press. The requirement for any information about the case became all consuming for them and they became vulnerable to many of the shameful techniques associated with the less ethical end of the industry. With such a large enquiry team it was difficult to keep the lid on things, but the integrity of the enquiry team held.

The days passed and still no obvious suspect was identified. The team was approaching the point of investigating a "sticker". Much worse, they had the press and the higher echelons of New Scotland Yard on their backs. The only lead was a witness who had seen a man washing his hands in a ditch close to the scene at the relevant time. High hopes were placed on the results of the examination particularly from DNA. The crime scene examiner had identified what he believed to be seminal fluid staining on the victim's underclothing. The swabs were currently undergoing analysis.

Amongst the first officers at the scene was one with a police dog. The dog traced a route from the murder, alongside a drainage ditch (where the earlier mentioned possible suspect had been seen washing his hands) to a wall. The wall was the common boundary and on the other side was Putney Vale Cemetery. It would not have been too difficult for any person of reasonable fitness to scale the wall and fence and gain access to the cemetery. Two further witnesses were found who distinctly heard the sounds of somebody crashing through the undergrowth on the cemetery side. Unfortunately, whoever caused the commotion was not within the sight of the witnesses.

Gloomy news reached the incident room, the anticipated DNA result proved negative. There was a tiny amount of cellular material but the laboratory was unable to raise a DNA profile from it. The investigating team were left with an open investigation into a murder of national interest with no concrete clues as to who was responsible.

The partner of Rachel, Andre had made a short impassioned appeal at a press conference after officially identifying the body of the woman he loved. He pleaded for anyone who had any information about the killer to come forward. He then said prophetically, "This person has to be found before someone else is killed and another family destroyed."

The investigating team had to get on with what they had. A detailed search was carried out in the vicinity of the murder and along the track taken by the man the witness saw washing his hands. No weapon was recovered, but footprints were discovered. They were a mixture of training shoes and working boots. It could be confirmed they had been made after the murder because it had rained heavily on the Tuesday night, the night before the murder and it had not rained since. Old marks had been blurred or eliminated, new marks were without any water in them and clear. The shoe marks were found by the ditch where the man had been seen washing his hands. All footwear prints were carefully preserved for comparison against any future suspect. Apart from the possibility of shoe and trainer marks there was no other scientific evidence to link the killer with the scene.

At the *post mortem* which was conducted by Dr Dick Shepherd the weapon used to inflict the wounds was estimated to be 1.5 cm in width at the hilt and 9 cm long. The hilt was square shaped, extending to 0.5 cm either side of the blade. The knife had a single cutting edge.

Witnesses were coming forward and giving descriptions of sightings. The witness who had seen a man in the vicinity of the drainage ditch on the edge of Putney Vale cemetery told how on her approach the man had ducked down into the stream as if washing his hands. He then walked-off in the direction of the cemetery. She was about 100 yards from him and described him as between 20 and 30 years of age, 6' tall with short collar length hair, wearing a cream sweater and loose blue jeans. He was carrying a black bag. The time of this sighting was significant as it could be given as 10.40 am, only five minutes after the estimated time of the murder.

Another significant witness was a mother Mrs Jane H, who was walking in the park with her three young children aged between three and 13. She had set off from the Windmill car park at 9.45 am. She saw something which immediately struck her as suspicious as she neared the Surrey Regiment memorial. A white man was walking towards her wearing dark trousers and a white button-up top, he had short dark brown hair and was clutching a dark coloured sports bag. He was about 5'10" tall and walked with an unusual stooping gait. She felt apprehensive as their paths were converging. The man was in his late twenties or early thirties and had a "babyish" sort of face. As they crossed paths she said, "Good morning." The man did not reply and averted his face. He walked on for a few feet more and appeared to slow in his stride, then walked on again. The time was (as to which she was insistent) 10.10 am. She carried on with her family to the Curling Pond and was sitting by it when she saw the same man returning. Another woman appeared, an attractive blond, on her left (later identified as a police officer's wife) the man changed direction and started to follow the new attraction. Mrs H was absolutely sure it was the same man. He was wearing a white button-up shirt and walked with a distinctive stoop. She felt concerned for the woman he appeared to be following and looked at her watch. It was 10.17 am.

At 10.23 am the same man appeared again, he walked around the Curling Pond and took off in the direction of where Rachel's body was later found. She noted that now he had a thin strap or belt around his waist and over the top of his shirt. Mrs H watched him disappear through a gap in the trees. This sighting was extremely significant. Another witness had seen Rachel and Alex walking towards Windmill Wood at 10.20 am.

Alex, although very young, had managed a description. This had to be tempered against his age but he did describe the assailant as wearing a white top.

At 10.30 am another witness saw a man crouching, washing his hands in the stream, she could not see his face but he was wearing a "cream or white top." He headed off in the direction of Putney Vale Cemetery, the same path as picked up by the police dog.

A Photofit was made. The witness who had seen the man three times described it as a very good likeness. The Photofit was proven to be a decisive factor when a local man, Colin Stagg was identified as being a good match. Stagg lived alone near the common. He had already entered the enquiry apart from being propped-up by members of the public as resembling the Photofit. He had been stopped by a police constable on the day of the murder at about mid-day trying to get onto the common by the cemetery underpass. Further information revealed that Stagg was a regular user of the common where he was often to be seen walking his dog.

Rachel Nickell.

CHAPTER 25

The Cases Collide ... But No-one Knows It

As the Rachell Nickell enquiry progressed the investigators were confronted by the same problem as had struck the Bisset investigation in the south east of London. There was no firm suspect. Time was slipping by and extreme pressure was being exerted by the media who had taken up the Nickell case. The pressure was being felt in the higher echelons of New Scotland Yard. The Association of Chief Police Officers (ACPO) came up with the suggestion that the team utilise the services of an offender profiler.

The current most experienced and successful of these was Paul Britton. Naturally, eyes turned towards him. Britton was currently working in Leicestershire at the Trent Regional Psychology Service. His reputation for quietly assisting police in offences of stranger attacks went before him. Paul Britton's profiles had led to the solving of some high profile murder cases and he had built a reputation on his methodical science-based approach which did not impinge on or take over the investigation. He had broadened his knowledge by liaison with others in the same field in America and, more importantly, had given both oral and written evidence to the Crown Court where he was recognised as an expert witness.

The Nickell team had nothing to lose. Paul Britton was contacted and agreed to assist. He was thoroughly briefed at the Wimbledon incident room and visited the scene of the attack on Wimbledon Common. Armed with as much information as he could glean from the circumstances, the victim and the scene of attack, Britton retired to Leicestershire to ponder. He concluded that the killer was one of a small group of people who had developed a predatory, sexual psychosis. This rare group have strong sexual needs but have not developed any self-esteem or social confidence.

This may be caused by ridicule or rejection in earlier relationships. When linked this can lead to a life of sexual inadequacy and loneliness.

An even smaller sub-group of this type may harbour resentment and a need grows within them to blame others for their predicament. They begin to develop a private fantasy world where they have the power and control. As their fantasies escalate they need more and more energy to satisfy their craving for sexual release. Their fantasies will gradually be transferred to real situations. He (for they are nearly always male) will follow women who resemble his fantasy. This process may go on for months as he pounds the streets, alleyways and peers into windows. Eventually he takes more and more risks. This is demonstrated in increased violence towards his victims.

He was without doubt a stranger to Rachel Nickell and knew he was taking an enormous risk but the circumstances were in his favour. There was limited cover, he knew his escape routes. Rachel paid the ultimate price for her attacker's pent up frustrations and aberrational fantasies. Paul Britton went on to give a profile of the killer. It was to prove eerily prophetic when later matched against Robert Napper; unfortunately without an actual suspect to compare against it wasn't immediately of any use. Not surprisingly the Nickell team did not associate the profile with that of the uncaught Green Chain Walk rapist who had until recently been operating in south east London. All the offences on the other side of London had been concentrated in the area of Plumstead and Eltham over 20 miles away. There was a pattern of increased violence, but nothing to compare with the murderous attack on Rachel.

The last known rape on 24th May 1992 did have similarities to the Nickell attack. Both victims were of similar age, appearance and stature. Both were with their very young children. In both cases a knife was used. One witness to Rachel's possible attacker saw what she thought was a ligature around the suspect's waist, over his shirt. The rape victim in Eltham was overpowered with a ligature. The violent attack on the last rape victim in Eltham used violence in the extreme but nothing to compare with that used against Rachel.

The last sex attack was almost three months prior to the Nickell murder. Napper, it was subsequently established, replenished his stock of hunting knives on 13th July 1972, just two days before the Nickell murder. Discounting the strange accosting of the woman on the bus in Woolwich which happened on 19th August 1992 no further offences, up until the murders of Samantha and Jazmine on the 3rd November 1993, could be attributed to Napper.

Paul Britton supplied the following profile of the man responsible for the murder of Rachel Nickell:

He will be aged between 20 and 30 years.

He will have practiced the offence but it will probably be his first killing.

He will have poor heterosocial skills and an inability to relate to women on an ordinary level.

He will have a history of failed or unsatisfactory relationships. If any.

In addition to his sexual deviation, it would be likely he suffers from some form of sexual dysfunction, i.e. no erection or ejaculation control.

He would be attracted to some form pornography which would play a role in his sexual fantasy life, some of it violent.

He will not be more than of average intelligence and education.

He will be single and leading a relatively isolated life.

If he is employed it will be in an unskilled or labouring occupation.

He will live either with a parent or alone in a bed-sit or flat.

He will have solitary hobbies and interests and these will be of an unusual nature and may include martial arts or photography.

He will probably not have access to a car.

He will live locally within easy walking distance of Wimbledon Common and will be thoroughly familiar with it.

There is a significant probability he has a history of sexual-offending. This may not include previous conviction.

Britton concluded with an ominous postscript:

"In my view it is almost inevitable that this person will kill another young woman at some point in the future as a result of the strong deviancy and aggressive fantasy urges."

Britton explained further that there are thousands of socially inept, lonely, unattractive, isolated men. However, the above profile would narrow the field. Looking back at it is a fascinating exercise. In most aspects it faithfully and accurately describes Robert Napper. One year later on 3rd November 1993, Napper would prove Mr Britton correct in his prediction that the killer of Rachel Nickell would murder another young woman. Unfortunately, as in all subjective profiles it only takes one wayward deduction to throw the direction of the investigation. In this case it was the prediction that offender would live within easy reach of Wimbledon Common.

On the 28th August 1992 (only six weeks after the Nickell murder) was when Napper was contacted for the first time by the Green Chain Walk rape Operation Eccleston team to attend Eltham Police Station for elimination through a blood sample. Napper, according to a witness who shared the same house at 189 Well Hall Road, Eltham had his bags packed as if ready to leave. As this was only six weeks after the Nickell murder it is little wonder that Napper took fright and packed his bags. He no doubt thought police were onto him for the murder in Wimbledon.

On the 24th September, having avoided giving a blood sample on two occasions, Napper took off and moved to 63 Reidhaven Road, Plumstead. It was whilst at this address that Napper was arrested for trying to have Metropolitan Police Service crests printed, and the search of his room revealed the .22 firearm with ammunition, a crossbow, a quantity of knives, a listening device and correspondence which included the *A to Z* containing the Richmond Park Isabella Plantation marking and the stolen gym fitness card for the young lady in Eltham, reported missing on 22nd September 1992, whose address was also marked in his *A to Z*. This was not linked by the investigators as a possible connection to the Green Chain rapes. As a result of all this Napper commenced a prison sentence on 2nd December 1992 which was to last 25 days.

The significance of the markings in the *A to Z* and the stolen gym card were not connected by the local CID officers at Plumstead to the Green Chain rapist. Napper began his short sentence and the property from the case, including the *A to Z*, was booked into the property office at Plumstead to gather dust and await eventual disposal.

Two months into the Rachel Nickell enquiry and there were still no positive leads. The team made a decision to try the time-honoured route of making an appearance on *Crimewatch* hosted by Nick Ross which had produced some good results for otherwise stuck crime investigations in the past. The programme aired in mid-September, just before the second request was made by the enquiry team of Operation Eccleston for Napper to provide a blood sample for elimination.

The edition of *Crimewatch* caused a sensation and produced over 800 responses from the public. Amongst the callers were three who all gave the name of an individual who frequented Wimbledon Common, lived locally and resembled the Photofit of the man seen washing his hands. The name given was Colin Francis Stagg. Of all the information received, Stagg was the standout. Nobody contacted *Crimewatch* with the name Robert Napper.

Records were checked and it was seen that Stagg had already been mentioned in the enquiry. He had been stopped by a police constable on the common at about mid-day on the day of the murder. The officer had given the stop a low profile marker because Stagg was in fact entering the common, not leaving it. When questioned he told the officer he had been on the common earlier in the day between 8 am and 8.30 am. Checks showed that Stagg had a brief, petty criminal record and that he lived close to Wimbledon Common, albeit on the Richmond Park side of the A3 on the Roehampton Estate (coincidentally as close to Isabella Plantation as to Wimbledon Common).

Two officers were dispatched to keep observation on Stagg's flat. Early the following morning at 8.30 Stagg appeared on his balcony giving the observing officers an uninterrupted view. One of them, Detective Constable Bill Lyle called excitedly into the incident room, "Our Photofit has walked out. What do you want us to do?" The decision was made to arrest Colin Stagg and to hold him on suspicion of the murder of Rachel Nickell. Operation Edzel "had their man".

Meanwhile in south east London, the spate of rapes on the Green Chain Walk had come to an unexpected stop.

CHAPTER 26

The Lead-up to Another Murder

Robert Napper's behaviour towards the end of 1992 was becoming ever more bizarre. Subsequent to the second request for a blood sample from him he moved to 63 Reidhaven Road, Plumstead. He would not have known how fate had been twisted in his favour and decisions were being made around the rape enquiry which would ensure his safety. At another level he was being discussed at his place of work at the Woolwich Arsenal as being very odd, often seen talking to himself and becoming increasingly paranoid about others on the workforce spying on him. Female members of staff felt particularly uncomfortable in or near his presence and avoided him. Their interest quickly vanished when Serco finally shut down their operation at Woolwich. Napper was made redundant on 11th September 1992.

It was after his redundancy notice that the incident with the gym fitness card happened on or after the 22nd September and then he was arrested when trying to have Metropolitan Police notepaper printed which resulted in the search of his flat and the finding of the .22 Erma pistol and ammunition, leading to a short prison sentence taking him into the New Year of 1993.

Meanwhile, DI Pedder interviewed Colin Stagg under caution at Wimbledon Police Station in the presence of Stagg's solicitor. Colin Stagg was cooperative and talkative. Prior to the interview Pedder had contacted Paul Britton, informed him of Stagg's arrest and given a brief background of the man in question. Reflecting on Britton's profile of the killer, many of the suggested parameters coincided perfectly. Britton was at Towers Hospital, Leicester and the consultation was by telephone. DI Pedder was advised to tread softly, to gain Stagg's confidence, to relate to his hobbies and then build on that. Britton was emphatic that he could not advise Pedder directly on Stagg as he himself had not seen or interviewed him. The advice he was giving was purely on the offender profile.

The interview took place over two days. Colin Stagg was cooperative and gave a wealth of personal information. His interest in painting (there were several of his own works in his flat), in backpacking and being able to live off the land he qualified by saying he would never kill a living creature and did not think he could bring himself to skin a dead one. He owned a knife which he kept in case he ever had to do it. He mentioned how he still felt guilt at having killed woodlice with a magnifying glass when he was aged about ten. He was aged 29 and lived alone. He played the guitar, but only for his own amusement. His mother had walked out on the family when he was 12 and he had subsequently been close to his father who died in 1986. He kept a dog, Brandy, which he exercised every day. He didn't use public houses and kept to himself.

He was then questioned on his movements on the day of the murder. He remembered the day well. It had stuck in his memory for various reasons, the first being that he had woken with a splitting headache, the type of which he had not had since his teenage years. He had breakfast and did a little necessary shopping, then at 8.30 am he took Brandy out for his regular walk on Wimbledon Common. Stagg gave the interviewing officer a detailed account of his route on the common using a plan provided. It took him through the underpass under the A3, past Scio Pond, Wandsworth and then on to the Surrey Regiment war memorial where it was his habit to feed the resident ravens. He reversed the journey back to his flat arriving at about 9.15 am.

When asked if he could remember seeing any other people on the common at that time he recalled seeing two dog walkers, a man and a woman on the Richmond side of the underpass. He had said "Good morning" to them both. The woman replied, the man didn't. He would normally take a longer walk but, as he still felt unwell, he wanted to get home and rest. He was wearing jeans, white Dunlop tennis boots, a black T-shirt and a black leather jacket. Having arrived back home at Ibsley Gardens, he fell asleep on the settee. He was woken from his slumber at between 10.30 am and 11 am by the sound of a helicopter tracking back and forth over the common. He still didn't feel well but having noticed the weather had brightened he donned a pair of cut down jeans, his black T-shirt, Dunlop tennis boots with white socks and a pair of sunglasses. He walked with his dog to the second underpass, a slightly different route from his early morning one, where he was prevented from entering the common by a police officer. The officer told him the common was being cleared as a "girl" had been murdered.

He walked back along Bessborough Road where he took the time to discuss the events on the common with the butcher, this was between 11.40 am and 12 o'clock. He then went home again. He did not know Rachel Nickell and saw no-one answering her description with a small child on the day of the murder. When asked if he could hand over the Dunlop trainers he said that he had binned them two days before because they were worn out and one of the heels had dropped off. He described which bin he had thrown them into.

He was asked about his Pagan beliefs and why he had one of his rooms in his flat painted black, with a pentagram and other symbols. Stagg explained about the Wicca religion and the misconception it was linked to Satanism. He believed all life was precious (Not the answer DI Pedder anticipated or wanted to hear).

The interview had thrown up many questions but very few answers. Colin Stagg was undoubtedly a "good" suspect. He matched many of the criteria of the offender profile supplied by Paul Britton. He had given a believable story of his activities on the day during questioning but had no alibi for the time of the murder at 10.30 am. His appearance matched the Photofit and description of the man seen washing his hands to an uncanny degree, even down to the stooping walk.

Stagg flew to the top of Operation Edzel as their main and only suspect. A witness, Mrs Lillian A knew Stagg casually. They often passed whilst walking their respective dogs and lived near to one another. She described him as a quiet man who always wore a black/navy T-shirt and jeans. On the day of the murder she saw him outside his flat at about 12.30 pm. He seemed unusually animated and excited. He asked her if she had heard of the murder and she said, "Yes".

He then said something which she thought was rather odd. "I often used to stand there on the top of the hill and look down to where it happened." Lillian wondered to herself how he knew where exactly it had happened. Stagg then told her he had missed the murder by only ten minutes. In his interview he had told police he was back home by 9.30 am, a full hour before the murder. Lillian was perturbed by Stagg's unusual reaction to the news of the murder. She described how he appeared as if he had just bathed and was wearing what looked like new clothes, he was wearing a white T-shirt, white shorts and trainers.

The meeting played on Lillian's mind and she telephoned her daughter to discuss it. Her daughter advised her to call the police, advice which she followed. She heard nothing from the enquiry team and Lillian patiently waited until the 17th September when she saw the publicised Photofit. The resemblance to Colin Stagg struck her immediately and she went round to where he lived to note down his house number. It was whilst she was approaching Stagg's address that she witnessed his arrest. She made herself known to the arresting officers and when they returned to the police station they read her earlier message, only then did they realised her significance as a possible witness.

Even more damningly, another witness came forward, Mrs Susan G. Susan had seen the *Crimewatch* programme and recalled the day of the murder. It had stuck in her mind because her mother-in-law was staying with her. Her mother-in-law was fretting about collecting her pension and Susan took her usual morning walk earlier to facilitate this. She remembered leaving the common via the Putney Vale underpass at 9.25 am. She was positive about the time because of needing to return home for her mother-in-law's pension.

As she was leaving the common she saw Colin Stagg (whom she knew well) entering it. She described him as wearing a white T-shirt (contradicting Lillian's description of a black T-shirt when she first saw him that day) and blue jeans; he appeared to be wearing a black bum bag. Colin had his dog Brandy with him. They acknowledged each other by waving as they normally did and Colin carried on onto the common going in the direction of the Windmill. When Susan first saw Stagg, Brandy was off the lead and Colin put him on it as he knew one of Susan's two dogs could be aggressive.

Just as the team felt they were stalling, they had been gifted a prime suspect. Colin Stagg fitted the Photofit to perfection. He had been seen on the morning of the murder wearing a white top and blue jeans and carrying a black bag, just as the man described by a witness Mrs Jane H washing his hands in the stream at 10.23 am. He appeared to have lied about the time he visited the common. In his story to DI Pedder he had said he was leaving the common at 9.30, whereas the witness Susan, who knew him well, saw him entering the common at that time. He knew the common in fine detail and was familiar with all entries and exits.

The interviews resumed with renewed hope but Stagg adamantly stuck to his story, pleading his innocence to the frustrated interviewing officers who were becoming increasingly sure they had their man.

Time for an extension of detention was applied for to arrange an identity parade. The press interest was now intense with a crowd of reporters and photographers encamped around Wimbledon Police Station. It was important to conduct the identity parade before photographs of Stagg were splashed all over the press. On Sunday 19th September identity parades were held at Brixton Police Station.

Mrs Jane H picked out Colin Stagg as the man dressed in the white top carrying a black bag she had seen washing his hands in the stream at 10.23 am. The same man she had seen at 10.10 am and 10.17 am. Further consultation was made with Paul Britton who suggested showing Stagg a photograph of the murder scene in interview, the rationale being that if he was in denial and refusing to accept he had committed such a terrible crime, the showing of a photograph would shock him into confessing. A none too graphic photograph was selected and duly shown to Stagg. It produced virtually no reaction.

The only thing to come out of the long interviews was Stagg's sudden admission that just after the murder he had "flashed" at a woman on Wimbledon Common. It seems bizarre that he should make such an unsolicited admission. It had no connection with the murder of Rachel Nickell other than pointing to one of the traits in Britton's suggested psychological profile, i.e. that the offender would have a history of offending, although maybe not accompanied by criminal conviction or equivalent seriousness. Another tick in the box against Stagg in the eyes of the investigators.

The time was approaching when a decision needed to be made whether to charge Stagg or release him. Here was the dilemma. Stagg had been identified as the man seen near to where the murder happened at the relevant time. If Susan G was to be believed, he was entering not leaving the common at 9.30 am which indicated he was lying to protect himself. He strongly matched the Photofit. He walked with a pronounced stoop. This was all evidence against Colin Stagg, but, it was circumstantial. The risk was that to charge would lead inevitably to eventual dismissal and it would be impossible to recover from that.

Stagg was charged with the lesser offence of indecency to which he had volunteered and released on police bail concerning the offence of murder, He was kept in custody overnight to appear at Wimbledon Magistrates' Court for the offence of indecent exposure. The appearance in court created a media frenzy. To a packed courtroom Stagg pleaded guilty to the exposure offence and was fined £200 with £20 costs. He was then free to go. He left the court via the rear entrance but the press were waiting. He made a quick statement proclaiming his innocence and hoping the killer would be found quickly. He then knocked over a cameraman's tripod and, sticking-up two fingers to the remaining media hounds, he strode off, in a perfect stoop.

CHAPTER 27

Convinced but not Convincing

Throughout 1993 Robert Napper continued his descent into madness. He managed to keep this from everyone by withdrawing more and more into himself. He lived alone and no longer visited any family members. He had no social outlets and built up a fantasy world of spats with the IRA, personal interviews with the queen and awards of Nobel Peace Prizes. None of these delusions were shared with anyone. They were however reinforced by his fascination with firearms, knives and combat magazines.

Since his arrest on firearm offences and his subsequent short prison sentence at the end of 1992, Napper had managed to avoid further contact with the police, with the exception of his stop in Rutherglen Road when he was suspected of being a Peeping Tom. He remained unemployed throughout the first part of 1993 until the 16th September when he secured employment as a machine operator/packer at Cryspecs, London SE18. On the 29th September he was asked to leave as he was found unsuitable. Specifically he was incapable of sticking labels onto the correct packages. He remained unemployed until 4th February 1994. It was during this period of unemployment, on 3rd November 1993, that he murdered Samantha and Jazmine Bisset.

By the time Napper's madness had driven him to murder Samantha and Jazmine the Wimbledon enquiry was locked into the belief that Colin Stagg was their man. The early warnings by Paul Britton that, after the introduction of an undercover detective, he would either damn or eliminate himself were proving to be a grey area of interpretation. There followed a bizarre sequence of events involving contact and correspondence between Colin Stagg and Lizzie James, an undercover police officer, to persuade Stagg to admit to Rachel's murder through feigned friendship. On the 22nd of May Stagg wrote her a letter in which he referred to the Nickell murder and his part in it. It included the line, "I could have lied to you about the murder, and say I did it, just to be with you." This setback was seen merely as Stagg showing caution.

Paul Britton predicted that if this were true there would be no further communication. If it wasn't true he would either admit to being involved in Rachel Nickell's murder or invent something completely different which would match Lizzie James' story of her being involved in murder in her past. Three days later, on the 25th May, during a telephone conversation, Stagg admitted to Lizzie James that he and a cousin had strangled a little girl in the New Forest when he was aged 12. The police scoured all their records. The story was an obvious lie. The correspondence continued through June, and Stagg continued to lay out his sexual fantasies to Lizzie James but came no nearer to any admission regarding any knowledge of the Nickell murder.

The 26 week deadline for the operation was approaching. It was decided to take a more proactive approach and Lizzie James wrote to Stagg a letter in which she described walking with him in woodland where, as they start to kiss, they are approached by a young blonde woman whom Stagg invites to join in their sex session. In the fantasy Stagg produces a knife with which he makes a small cut in one of the woman's nipples. The episode, Stagg is told by Lizzie James, has the effect of making her sexually-aroused.

Now, 23 weeks into the sting, another meeting in Hyde Park was arranged for 29th June. The pair occupied a couple of deck chairs next to the Serpentine. Stagg brought a bottle of wine which he opened with a Swiss Army knife. Lizzie James turned the conversation to the Nickell killing. Stagg told Lizzie that if she spent the weekend with him he could show her where the murder happened. Lizzie James then played her trump card. "So that's the thing you were talking about ... You said you had been arrested for that thing on the common." Stagg explained in detail his arrest and interview and how the police believed he had committed the murder.

Lizzie James interjected, "I wish you had done it, knowing you got away with it. I'd think, that's brilliant. I wish you had. Screw 'em."

Stagg went on to talk about his police interview and how they had shown him a photograph of the murder victim. How she was stabbed 49 times and was almost decapitated. She asked if the victim had been raped and he replied, "Yeah, he done everything." He described the photograph he had been shown by the police. "She was lying down on the ground, you know, like when you are a baby, sort of curled up." He told Lizzie James that the sight of the photograph had sexually-aroused him and he went on to give a detailed description of her body position and genitalia, including the position of her hands, but he then reiterated he had not killed her and was back home in bed by 9.30 am, nursing his headache.

The results of the meeting were discussed with Paul Britton. The feeling was that Stagg was about to confess. This was reinforced by his description of the body position, which all agreed he could not have known from the one photograph he had been shown during interview. The investigating team had staked everything on Stagg confessing to the undercover officer. They had persuaded the Top Floor at New Scotland Yard to back them. Reputations were on the line.

Colin Stagg telephoned Lizzie James on the 1st July. He suggested a meeting on Wimbledon Common on a weekday when it was quieter. He suggested they both strip off and he would produce a knife whilst masturbating over her. He would show her exactly where the murder happened and where he was at the time. Convinced that Stagg was about to make a confession to undercover police officer Lizzie James, the team were keen to act as she, DCI Wickerson and DI Pedder drove north for another meeting with Paul Briton to discuss the forthcoming, in their minds, crucial liaison between Stagg and James. En route the trio stopped for breakfast at a service station on the M1. DCI Wickerson's attention was attracted by a newspaper banner headline in the news stand. The *Daily Star* had a front page spread with the headline "I DIDN'T KILL RACHEL NICKELL."

The storyline followed in which, during an interview with a reporter from the *Daily Star*, Colin Stagg emphatically denied murdering Rachel. He reiterated his uncorroborated alibi that he was back at his flat by

9.30 am. The meeting with Paul Britton took on a different slant to the one planned. All agreed that Stagg's unsolicited pronouncement of innocence in a national newspaper did not help their cause.

Paul Britton was sanguine. He pointed out that the anniversary of the murder was approaching and there was bound to be press interest resulting in Stagg becoming more cautious. He proposed that Lizzie James get in touch with Stagg. Take the line she was upset with the story insofar as he had spoken to the press. Tell him now that she had opened-up about her secrets to him, she felt in jeopardy. The next step was to put the ball in Stagg's court. Colin Stagg was due to telephone Lizzie James that afternoon. The phone call happened at the allocated time. Lizzie James went on the offensive accusing Stagg of being "the kind of person that goes to the press."

She was upset at the damage it might do to their relationship. Stagg was unfazed. "You've gotta stand up to these people ... I'm just trying to clear my name you know." The telephone call was followed two days later by a letter from Stagg. It was another fantasy written in a similar theme to those before. Sex with Lizzie James, including a third party male on the grass near a tree on a warm summer's evening. During sex he pricks her throat with a knife causing her to bleed.

Paul Briton's assessment of the fantasy was of it suggesting someone suffering a serious sexual deviance. He added, crucially, "I note the close resemblance of Mr Stagg's account to various elements present in the murder of Rachel Nickell." At a stroke the goalposts had been moved. A confession was no longer the underlying reason for the sting. The idea had now mutated into Stagg's perceived psychological profile matching that of the killer. The obvious danger of this concept was that in such an arbitrary, inexact science, the believers, especially the new converts are tempted to make leaps of judgement to confirm facts and give shrugs of dismissal when the facts do not fit.

One more meeting was set up at The Dell, Hyde Park on 21st July. It was going to be make or break and was almost to the day 26 weeks since the first letter of the sting had been sent. During this meeting Stagg made it obvious he wanted to progress from fantasising about sex with Lizzie James to the actual act. Lizzie James was direct and made it clear she wanted a man like someone who had killed Rachel. He talked about Rachel being decapitated (something which did not actually happen). He gave more descriptions of the position of Rachel's body, which he could not have known from the one photograph he had been shown in his police interview, but denied he was responsible for the murder. In reply to her stories of ritual murders Stagg could only say, "I can't compete with that." Lizzie James ended the meeting, Stagg watched her go and made no attempt to follow her. The sting was over.

The meetings at the CPS, the Attorney General's office and New Scotland Yard went into overdrive. Consultations were held at every level. There was no doubt in everyone's mind that not to charge Colin Stagg, if he were Rachel's murderer, would allow him the freedom to strike again. The enquiry now hinged on points of law. It was the investigators contention that the evidence was contained in the psychological profile. This profile reinforced the facts that Stagg was on the common on the morning of the murder, something he himself admitted. The witness, Mrs Jane H, positively identified him as the person she had seen in the vicinity of the murder at the relevant time. Something that Stagg denied, keeping to his story that he was at home by 9.30 am. If she were to be believed, Stagg was lying.

The enquiry team disbelieved Stagg's story and pushed for a charge. Nobody ever asked, where, in all of these crucial sightings, was Stagg's constant companion, his dog Brandy. Although the psychological profile identified many likenesses to Stagg, there were others which did not fit so neatly. Stagg was an intelligent man belying the profile's prediction that the killer would be of below average intelligence. He insisted he was wearing a black T-shirt (his habitual garb) when he went onto the common on the morning of the killing, corroborated by one witness. The man seen in the vicinity of the murder was wearing a white or cream top.

By the second week of August a decision had been reached at the highest level and filtered down to the team. Authority was given to charge Colin Stagg with the murder of Rachel Nickell. On the 17th August Stagg was arrested and taken to Wimbledon Police Station where he was formally charged. It had been a tremendous slog and a deal of hard work to get this far. It was far from over. Now it would be up to a jury to decide.

It would be their decision whether it was safe to allow Stagg back onto the streets and also for the judge whether or not the police introduction of psychological profiling was a proper way of offering evidence.

The pressure was really on for a resolution to be made over the killing of Rachel. The team had pushed and pushed. The top floor at New Scotland Yard had, after advice from lawyers, decided to give the go ahead to charge Stagg with murder. Stagg was now to be shoehorned into a fit, discrepancies were to be ignored. The possibility that he might *not* have done it became a secondary consideration with selective picking of the positives. Even Stagg's insistence that he was back at home at 9.30 am was construed as Stagg having told a lie and now being totally bound in sticking to it. If he changed his story he was doomed.

The possibility of Stagg telling the truth and the witness having made a mistake by identifying someone who looked uncannily like him was not given credence. Colin Stagg was remanded in custody which at least gave him a perfect alibi when the killer of Rachel Nickell struck again on the opposite side of London on the 3rd November 1993.

The Cases go to Court

During his interview after arrest and prior to charge Stagg elected to make "no comment" replies to all of DI Pedder's questions. This was a complete turn around from his early interviews when he was compliant and ready to answer all questions. At the culmination of the interview on 18th August 1993 he was charged with Rachel Nickell's murder. He remained in custody through 1993 and into 1994 awaiting trial.

The day after he was charged it became apparent that the investigating team had a problem. After the celebrations of the night before the tabloid press on the following morning of the 19th were full of lurid stories of the undercover operation. The team appeared to have a mole divulging information to the press. Now, on top of everything else, an internal investigation was initiated to discover who had leaked the information. The effect was to cast a shadow over the team and create what seemed to be an insidious lack of trust.

The uncanny parallels with the downmarket events in Plumstead continued with the appointment of counsel for the prosecution and defence. Representing the crown was Treasury Counsel Nigel Sweeney QC. For the defence, William Clegg QC. The same two leads who would eventually be called to handle the Robert Napper trial. At the heart of the prosecution case against Colin Stagg was:

- The evidence gleaned from the undercover operation proved by similar fact that Stagg was a very disturbed individual with the same form of sexually-deviant personality disorder as the killer of Rachel Nickell.

- That he had been identified by Mrs Jane H as the man she had seen carrying a black bag and behaving oddly at about the time of the killing.
- From Stagg's letter writing and other intelligence, proof could be assumed that Stagg was the Mrs Jane H suspect.
- QED Stagg was suffering from a rare psychotic disorder and had been identified as being near the scene at the time of the killing.

The legal system ground onwards and committal proceedings were scheduled for January 18th 1994. In the meantime the "no expense spared" ethos continued so it seems with DI Pedder and Paul Britton being flown to the United States of America for liaison with the Federal Bureau of Investigation (FBI) to study the many cases in America where psychological profiling had been successfully utilised.

Committal proceedings were eventually started on the 17th February at Wimbledon Magistrates' Court before a court packed with reporters from the press waiting to see if there was a case to be answered. The prosecution's junior counsel was William Boyce and for the defence James Sturman. When Colin Stagg made his appearance it was shocking to see the change in him. The stocky, muscular features had gone to be replaced by a thin vulnerable figure. The witnesses gave their testimony. Mrs G had seen Stagg, whom she knew, at around 9.30 am with his dog Brandy near the underpass. He was walking in the direction of the Windmill. He was wearing a white T-shirt and blue jeans. Mrs PF had seen a man aged 29 or 30 walking purposefully on the common near the scene at 9.30 am, he was carrying a black bag. Mrs AP described seeing a man washing his hands in a stream at 10.30 am, he was wearing a white or cream sweater. Neither Mrs AP nor Mrs PF had picked out Colin Stagg at the identity parade.

Mrs Jane H described how she had seen a white man, 5' 10" tall, wearing a white, long-sleeved shirt with a collar. He was carrying a dark-coloured bag by its handles. They passed each other. Shortly afterwards she saw the man again on the far side of the Curling Pond following a woman before disappearing into some trees. In a few minutes the same man reappeared, this time he had a thin belt around his waist over his shirt. She had provided police with the information from which they constructed an E-fit. The E-fit resulted in the first arrest of Stagg. Mrs Jane H picked-out Colin Stagg at the subsequent identity parade. She was positive it was the same man.

A succession of witnesses were examined including local people who had seen Stagg at various times carrying a black bag. Then the pathologist Dr Dick Shepherd gave his evidence. He was asked if he had had any contact with Paul Britton. He replied, "I have never met Paul Britton at any time, I have not discussed any aspect of this case with him. I have seen no reports prepared by him." Of the attack, he deduced it was in four phases.

- One, the initial attack, striking fatal blows to the neck.
- Two, the victim was moved or staggered to the base of the tree with the killer lunging at her body with the knife.
- Three, Rachel's lower clothing was removed whilst still raining down blows.
- Four, the killer sexually violated his victim.

There were 49 stab wounds in all, at least 13 inflicted after death. It did not necessarily follow that the assailant was covered in blood as most of the original loss would have been soaked into her upper clothing and onto the ground. Swabs were taken but unfortunately no samples offered a trace from which a DNA-reading could be made. It did not appear the attacker had ejaculated and there were no traces of skin under her fingernails. In fact, there were no defensive wounds, those resulting from the victim fending-off the attack, at all.

On the second day Paul Britton was called. He was asked to define the discipline of offender profiling. He explained how it was well-established and widely used since the late-1940s based on medical principles and had gained a Royal Charter in 1965. From his experience there could be no doubt that the killer of Rachel Nickell was one of a tiny number of perverts. He then went on to state he had devised the covert operation involving Lizzie James with the purpose of implicating or eliminating Colin Stagg. The operation contained the specific proviso that if Stagg did not react in the manner expected he would eliminate himself. Britton then took a step further, committing himself. He said Stagg's sexuality was on a par with the offender profile he had constructed after the killing and before Stagg became a suspect.

James Sturman immediately saw his chance. He proposed that the profile was not scientific but rather an unsupported and speculative treatise based on Paul Britton's instincts. He launched an attack, "Is Colin Stagg mentally-ill?" Britton could only reply." I don't know, I've never examined him."

"Does he suffer from any abnormality within the terms of the Mental Health Act?" Again the only response open was, "I can't tell you that."

The probing into the value of offender profiling continued into the next day, with Britton feeling more and more under attack. He was asked to explain the particular type of deviancy which would lead to the sufferer murdering Rachel Nickell. An explanation was given that the condition tends to affect young men in their teens, arouses intense and violent fantasies for many years and finally manifests itself in a murderous attack at the age of around 28. The condition affects only a tiny proportion of a sub-group of the population, but those who are affected are a "walking time bomb". He continued, "I don't know if Mr Stagg is such a person. What I can tell you is that the operation I designed was specifically constructed so as to present whoever was to be the subject of the operation a series of ladders they would have to climb in a conceptual sense."

Sturman then asked, "Would you not agree Mr Britton, that there is a lot of academic concern about offender profiling?" Britton answered that there were "one or two" dissenting voices and it was certainly the case that the storing of case study files was still at an early stage. "But, as a consequence of work in this area, work is now being undertaken on behalf of the Home Office and the Association of Chief Police Officers towards the development of more powerful analytical tools."

He then repeated his assertion that the chances of two men with the same sexual deviancy being together in the same place at the same time was vanishingly remote.

The next witness was to be the undercover officer Lizzie James who gave her evidence from behind a wooden screen to shield her identity from the public. Her submissions were brief. She was not put under great pressure by James Sturman, with only one awkward question as to her reason for befriending Stagg. "Were you trying to see whether Mr Stagg would incriminate himself in the murder."

She replied with composure, "No. I was trying to find out if he was implicated or not." At the end of the hearing Sturman summed-up with a blistering attack on the prosecution case. He asserted that the whole operation was conducted around Colin Stagg's vulnerability and sexual immaturity, in his desperation to lose his virginity he would have written anything to get her into bed. He finished rather accurately.

"We simply do not know what lunatic was loose on the common that day. Mr Britton is trying to prove possible guilt by giving an opinion. You are being asked to create legal history."

Finally, stipendiary magistrate Terry English pronounced his decision that there was a case to answer and he committed the case for trial at the Central Criminal Court. An application for bail was refused and Colin Stagg was led away to Wandsworth Prison. Whilst Stagg contemplated his fate and the injustice of the justice system at Her Majesty's pleasure, Robert Napper took up employment at Glyndon Plastics on the Thamesmead Industrial Estate. Conveniently situated within a mile of his bed-sit at 135 Plumstead High Street, his hours of work were from 8 am to 8 pm Monday to Friday. After a reasonable start he began to waver. He went off sick on odd days without calling in. He was reprimanded for not clocking back in after his lunch break on several occasions. One of his supervisors was a woman, Geraldine Pullen. Whenever she had to talk to Napper about his work she felt he did not respond kindly to being told what to do by a woman. He worked at Glyndon Plastics until he was sacked the day before his arrest on 27th May 1994.

Without either investigation, concerning Rachel Nickell or Samantha and Jazmine Bisset, knowing how inextricably they were linked they danced a macabre dance through 1994 and toward trials at the Central Criminal Court; one case under the glare of press interest, the other chugging along with a team of five on the outskirts of London, both with the same murderer, only one of them with a guilty man.

The trial date for Colin Stagg was the first to fall and was listed for 5th September 1994. After the old-style committal in February and before the trial, Nigel Sweeney QC stood down as the leading counsel for the prosecution. His place was taken by John Nutting QC, another Treasury Counsel. He took up the case with less than a month to go before trial but soon had a grasp of its complexities. His initial enthusiasm however began to be tested as the trial date loomed.

Sweeney now had more time to concentrate on the more obscure case of Samantha and Jazmine Bisset. He did so little realising he was now prosecuting not only the killer of Samantha and Jazmine but the killer of the victim of the case he had just dropped, of Rachel Nickell.

CHAPTER 29

The Trial of Colin Stagg

I t is dizzying to try and follow the sequence of events in the saga of these unknowingly linked investigations. A pause will be taken to consider the chronological order of events:

10/08/1989 the first rape of a young mother in her house in Plumstead.

10/03/1992 the first of a series of three sexual assaults which become progressively more violent on the Green Chain Walk, SE London.

18/03/92 The third sexual assault/rape.

24/05/92 The fourth and most violent rape of a young mother on open land in the presence of her child.

15/07/1992 The murder of Rachel Nickell on Wimbledon Common.

19/08/92 The stalking of a young woman at Woolwich Common.

28/08/92 The first request for a blood sample from Napper.

17/09/92 The first arrest and interview of Colin Stagg for the murder of Rachel Nickell.

18/09/1992 The second request for blood from Napper.

March 93 Decision made to close Operation Eccleston, the Green Chain rape enquiry.

31/07/93 Napper stopped and questioned for peeping at the Rutherglen Road incident.

13/08/93 The second arrest and charge of Colin Stagg after which he remains in custody until his trial.

03/11/93 The murders of Samantha and Jazmine Bisset in Plumstead SE London.

27/05/94 Napper arrested for the murders of Samantha and Jazmine and linked to the Green Chain rape series.

05/09/94 Colin Stagg arraigned for trial at the Old Bailey.

14/09/94 The trial against Colin Stagg collapses and he walks free.

02/09/95 The trial of Robert Napper at the Old Bailey where he is convicted of rape and murder.

The Nickell team continued with their preparations for the forthcoming trial at the Central Criminal Court. They were feeling optimistic. A vast amount of work had been concentrated into solving a very difficult case and it had been achieved by the adoption of cutting-edge science, utilising untried methods, untried insofar as using the field of psychological profiling as evidence. The team had had their doubts but had received backing from the highest ranks in the police and confirmation of the legality of their theories from the sharpest legal minds within the Crown Prosecution Service and the judiciary.

Their euphoria and confidence received a blow when in March 1994 in Leeds, the culmination of a murder trial against Keith Hall resulted in his acquittal. Hall's wife Patricia had suddenly disappeared without trace after they had had a vociferous argument overheard by neighbours. Hall claimed that after the row Patricia had walked-out on him, driving off in their Ford Sierra. The car was later found abandoned with the driving position set up for the smaller Patricia. Unfortunately for Hall the car had been seen by a milkman who gave evidence that it was a man he had seen at the wheel. Despite intense searching, neither Patricia nor her remains were ever found. Hall gave a "no comment" interview to police on the advice of his solicitor. The police were stuck with strong suspicion but insufficient evidence. Six months afterwards a woman came forward to police. She had placed an entry in the local newspapers lonely hearts column. The case had received intense publicity locally and she recognised the name Keith Hall.

Police substituted the woman with an undercover police officer and set up a correspondence. The letters progressed to telephone calls and eventually the two met with the police officer "wired". Over the next five months the pair met five times. Hall fell completely for the officer and asked her to marry him. Her response was that she would always be afraid that Patricia might return home. At the final meeting Hall told her that there was no way his wife would ever be returning as he had killed her and disposed of her body in an incinerator.

The police pounced and Hall was arrested and charged with his wife's murder. Hall stood trial at Leeds Crown Court on the 12th March 1994. After days of legal argument the judge ruled that the evidence of the undercover officer, including the taped confession, was inadmissible. Hall was found not guilty and walked free from the court.

The result of the Hall case threw the Nickell lawyers into a state of unsure trepidation. Discussions were held, the facts were pored over as to how or if it would impact on the Nickell case. Police waited and held their breath. With great relief a decision was made that the Hall trial did not throw the Nickell case into jeopardy. It was a very different kind of operation in legal opinion and did not run along the same lines as the Nickell undercover operation.

With the Hall case there was a whiff of entrapment, whereas in Wimbledon the covert operation had been run under very different lines and was not designed to manipulate the suspect into making a confession. It was (and here comes the mantra) intended to allow him to either eliminate himself entirely or to further implicate himself by his own choice. It does require the services of an intellectual to ponder how this conclusion could ever have been reached. At least in the Hall case a clear confession had been drawn. It really is splitting hairs to cast the Nickell undercover operation in a superior light, dressing it up in baffling terminology. Treasury Counsel, the lead solicitors of the Crown Prosecution Service and the upper echelons of the Metropolitan Police Service pondered the legal niceties and the possible negative impact on the police service, or the possibility of being at the forefront of legal history (presumably with the attached career enhancing opportunities).

On the same March morning in the less salubrious environs of his bed-sit at 135 Plumstead High Street, Robert Napper prepared himself for work as a moulding operator at Glyndon Plastics, Thamesmead Industrial Estate. Little realising as he pressed the moulds that he was the other half of a "vanishingly small chance of two psychologically disturbed men being on Wimbledon Common at the same time" he had no notion that in another six weeks he would lose his freedom forever.

In the Rachel Nickell case, the final case conferences were held and the trial date approached; now with a slightly less optimistic air, a final case conference was held with leading prosecution counsel, now John Nutting QC in his chambers at Temple Bar.

Nutting asked Paul Britton directly, "If the evidence relating to Stagg's guilty knowledge were excluded, is your evidence sufficient basis to convict?" Britton without hesitation replied, "Of course it is not sufficient. I cannot say that Colin Stagg killed Rachel Nickell. I can only say that the probability of there being two people on Wimbledon Common that morning who suffered from the same extreme and violence-orientated sexual deviation is incredibly small."

John Nutting went on to explain that the defence would launch an all out attack on the evidence of Lizzie James in an attempt to make it inadmissible. He did not need to add, should they succeed the trial was all but over. If John Nutting feared the trial might turn into a disaster, he could not have envisaged in his worst nightmares just how big a catastrophe it would turn out to be. The British system of justice revels in theatrical drama. Every trial has its players, stars and bit parts, all governed by the robed and bewigged judge and taunted and teased by the begowned prosecution and defence. No doubt, it is a serious business but the panoply of rigid custom and form inevitably injects a feeling of comedy into the proceedings. Weeks and months of work in the build up can be dismissed at a stroke if the rules are not adhered to. Any notion that the *raison d'être* is justice is soon forgotten in the swirl of robes and gowns. Underlying it all and never to be forgotten by the unwary, is the terrible power the system wields.

Shortly after 10.30 on 5th September 1994 proceedings began before Mr Justice Harry Ognall in No. 1 Court. The defence team, William Clegg and James Sturman on the front bench next to the prosecution John Nutting and David Waters. The elite of the legal profession and all vastly experienced in the ways of the court. In the tiny dock which lay at the top of narrow stairs leading from the cells below stood Colin Stagg, looking thin and pale.

Just as soon as the trial began it was halted for legal argument, before the swearing in of a jury. Mr Justice Ognall decreed that he needed three days to read through the transcripts of the interviews. Eyebrows were raised, the court was dismissed. On 8th September the trial resumed. William Clegg laid out his arguments. He concentrated on the part played by Lizzie James. In his view she had clearly led Colin Stagg on. She had told him, "My imagination knows no bounds and 'normal' things are not enough." This was clearly intended to make Stagg believe she had uninhibited fantasies and was intended for Stagg to respond in kind, leading to admissions relevant to the Nickell murder.

If Colin Stagg did not respond as hoped, she would put him on short supply. If he did respond with a fantasy she would encourage more. She wrote that she had taken part in the ritual murder of a child. This did not produce the desired effect from Colin Stagg, i.e. he didn't try and trump her with the confession of murdering Rachel. She went so far as to tell Stagg that she wished he had been the one who had murdered Rachel. His response was a disappointing "I'm terribly sorry, but I didn't."

William Clegg addressed the judge. "It is difficult to imagine an operation more calculated to result in material which a court would hold as inadmissible." Clegg continued to attack the police operation. "It is our submission that this officer, Lizzie James, subjected Stagg to quite deliberate manipulation, designed to get him to incriminate himself." The court adjourned for lunch and resumed in the afternoon. This time it was John Nutting's turn. He wasted no time in arguing the premise of the operation. "The object was not to trick the defendant into making admissions but rather to investigate the defendant's sexual fantasies."

It was an uphill struggle as he widened the argument to include Paul Britton. He explained how Britton had submitted his profile of the killer before Stagg was identified. Subsequent to Stagg's arrest, Briton predicted fantasy and reality would merge and he would discuss the killing. The operation was controlled and interpreted he said by Britton at all stages and designed to give Stagg the opportunity to display his innocence.

He continued, "The evidence gathering nature of this operation is best illustrated as having value if interpreted by someone else, rather like a fingerprint obtained by a police officer only has value if evaluated by someone else." The legal arguments sallied back and forth for two days. Another adjournment for the weekend and the legal arguments continued on Monday morning but all could see it was not looking good for the prosecution.

On Monday morning William Clegg went relentlessly on the attack. He suggested the undercover operation conducted by the police was flawed, legally and morally and as such was unreliable and inadmissible. He suggested that the undercover officer, far from being passive, had encouraged, blackmailed and bribed Stagg into fitting himself into Paul Britton's profile. The judge adjourned the case until Wednesday when he declared he would deliver a judgment.

It was an uncomfortable two days for the police team. If the judge in the Hall case had been critical then the judgment delivered by Mr Justice Ognall was withering. The court hung on his every word.

"I would be the first to acknowledge the great pressure put on officers in the pursuit of this enquiry, but I'm afraid this behaviour betrays not merely an excess of zeal but a blatant attempt to incriminate a suspect by positive and deceptive conduct of the grossest kind."

He continued,

"A sustained enterprise to manipulate the accused, sometimes subtly, sometimes blatantly, and designed, by deception, to manoeuvre and seduce him to reveal fantasies of an incriminating character and to, wholly unsuccessfully admit the offence."

Then the *coup de grace*,

"If a police operation involves the clear trespass into impropriety, the court must stand firm and bar the way."

The judge continued in his highly critical vein of all aspects of the prosecution case eventually finishing at 11.45 am by declaring that Colin Stagg should now walk free. An outburst from the public gallery and Stagg was led down the steps to freedom. The court spilled-out in an orgy of shouts and shoving. After a few moments only quietness remained, but with the exception of a faint splash of water in the distance. What could it be? It was the sound of oars in the water. The hierarchy of the Metropolitan Police Service were rowing for shore.

The debacle of the trial left institutions and individual careers at risk. It took a little while for things to settle down, but at least New Scotland Yard escaped the main avalanche of criticism. They need not have worried about damage limitation exercises, the press would do their work for them. Their disdain was heaped upon the investigating team and more upon the justice system itself, but most of their scorn was reserved for Paul Britton whose no doubt genuine and well-meaning theories and involvement seemed to be imploding, at least in terms of admissible evidence in a criminal trial.

Colin Stagg (centre, holding paper) outside court after being acquitted.
Photo: PA.

CHAPTER 30

Suspicions Abound

Working conditions at Belvedere Police Station were far from unpleasant. The team rubbed along together well. DI Pearse often arrived at the office early. He was naturally under great pressure from many sides including retrospectively the Green Chain Walk rapes enquiry. No matter how you viewed it, the investigation had been cut short, too soon, too incomplete. There were many outstanding actions left undone or not satisfactorily resolved.

One morning Alan and Roger had been on an early morning enquiry and returned to Belvedere. As usual the station was quiet and after parking the car in the yard they entered the building via the back door. The door led to stairs, then up to the floor on which the incident room was. As they climbed the stairs they heard a raised voice coming from the incident room. DI Pearse was on the phone. The voice rose to a shout.

Alan and Roger entered the office and John Pearse looked up momentarily, furious so it seemed as he continued to remonstrate with the unfortunate listener at the other end of the phone. He looked-up, appearing to be a little embarrassed, and sat back in his chair, staring at the telephone as if it were an instrument of medieval torture. Roger broke the silence, "Do you want a brandy in your tea, guv?"

Many evenings were spent going over details with David Spens, junior counsel to Nigel Sweeney. The routine was that Spens would fax ahead his concerns in the form of "advice". Alan or Roger would dig out the details and the two of them would go through any problems. The results were either faxed back or produced at one of the many conferences. From the consensus, Alan raised further actions if necessary.

If David Spens ever had any suspicion that Napper could be responsible for the Rachel Nickell murder he kept them to himself. The fact that Nigel Sweeney had withdrawn from the Nickell case was never discussed or even raised as an interesting issue. Alan and Roger at that time were unaware that Sweeney had been initially appointed as prosecuting counsel for the Crown against Colin Stagg.

The suspicions of Alan and Roger that Napper was a reasonable suspect for the Nickell murder were buried under concerns for their own forthcoming trial. The preparation of disclosure to the defence alone took up a huge chunk of time. All documents had to be vetted first and redacted if necessary and there were a lot of them. The sheer weight of disclosure alone was enough to make the strongest investigator blanche. But it was necessary. Defence representatives had recently been very successful in using disclosure, or rather the lack of it, to have cases thrown out at court.

There was still an imbedded reluctance within the police to part with information which may assist the defence, this outlook could be a fatal flaw and result in the loss of a job. Alan was of the opinion to tell the defence everything unless it was forbidden under the sensitive material schedule, and only then if it could be defended. Too many cases had been lost of late by the defence finding out late in the day of either a possible alibi or the ignoring of other potential suspects.

By the time Christmas 1994 had been and gone, the case against Napper was at an advanced stage. The trial date was set for late-August 1995. The tidying-up operation continued. Further searches were conducted with Captain Bacon of the Royal Artillery for possible hiding places where Napper may have stashed trophies and where there may be further evidence to be found. More time was spent by Alan reading through all messages and actions from the beginning of the enquiry up to date. This exercise is essential in any complex enquiry. A message or written statement which may have passed muster as being of little importance when it entered the system can, on review when later shone under the light of a different context, produce valuable insights. The good investigator is constantly curious and forever revisiting old ground for new understanding.

Alan maintained constant contact with Margaret (who he now also knew as "Maggie") and Jack Morrison, keeping them up-to-date with the progress of the trial. He was only able to visit them on two more occasions when further enquiries had come to light which involved old acquaintances of Samantha who were resident in Scotland, mostly down the east coast, Peterhead, Aberdeen, Arbroath and Dundee. These visits were not entrusted to the local constabulary but were saved-up and made over two or three days after a flight to Aberdeen.

Margaret and Jack always made Alan most welcome in their house by the sea south of Stonehaven. He was struck by their calm dignity and support of the investigation. Alan explained how Napper had been charged with a series of rapes committed prior to the murder of Jazmine and Samantha. He painfully explained he considered that because of a mistake made in the rape enquiry Napper might have been arrested before Samantha and Jazmine were so cruelly taken. Jack as usual took the news phlegmatically, Margaret did not seem to understand fully but realised it could easily have been much different.

The collapse of the Rachel Nickell trial had not gone unnoticed in the small incident room in Belvedere. The case often came up in conversation during a relaxing pint after work in the Victoria pub, a short walk from the police station. The pub was run by Bob the brother of the comedian Jim Davidson. He was an ex-Navy man like Alan and they were able to swap a few salty tales whilst Roger, Peter Canavan and Alan tucked into the most amazing steak sandwiches.

One thing the sudden ending of the Colin Stagg trial had thrown-up was a proliferation of published photographs which included those of Stagg and the Photofit constructed by the witnesses. Back in the office Alan produced a folder in which they were displayed juxtaposed with the arrest photograph and Green Chain rape Photofit of Robert Napper.

"What do you think boys?"

The similarities were uncanny. Even the two Photofits could have been of the same man. The most extraordinary feature was the resemblance between the them. Peter looked at the pictures laughing. "Don't tell me you're thinking of going over there again."

"No. Not after the last knockback and after Roger went over with Banksy." The three of them looked at the pictures. Alan said, "Anyway the enquiry room will have shut down by now." Roger added, "In any event the last thing the job wants to hear now is another suspect, didn't they make a statement after the trial that they weren't looking for anyone else?"

Peter added, "Well we know that's code for they still believe he did it."

Roger leaned in. "I think it was her dad who said that."

Alan closed the folder. "We've enough to do at the moment to make sure we get our job home and dry, but I've got a nasty feeling about this and I can't just let it go."

As the day of the trial approached the conferences at the chambers of Nigel Sweeney QC became more frequent. They were generally attended by Micky Banks, Bryan Reeve, Roger, Alan and a CPS representative. Despite the pressures the meetings were always conducted in a friendly and patient manner. Sweeney proved to be a perfect gentleman with an encyclopaedic grasp of the case.

The trial date was put further back whilst a full mental assessment was made of Napper. There was a genuine fear that, because of his mental condition, the case might be lost by never having a trial. It could be lost insofar as he would be committed under the Mental Health Act without standing trial which is never a satisfactory conclusion for victims, their relatives and lastly but not least for the police.

As Peter pointed out in his succinct manner, "If they Nut and Gut him, some quack five years down the line will reckon they've cured him and the next thing you know he'll be back out on the streets."

Maybe an exaggeration but everybody knew where he was coming from.

 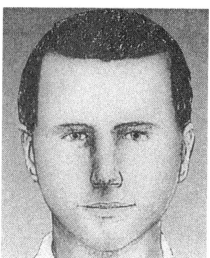

Left: Photofit of the Green Chain Walk rapist. Right: Artist's impression of a man seen near the Rachel Nickell murder scene.

Napper

CHAPTER 31

The Psychologists Have a Field Day

Napper was subjected to the examination of a string of eminent psychologists. He was examined at various times from February 1995 through to September 1995 by no less than five. For anyone studying the field of criminal psychosis Napper was a Heaven sent opportunity. Or, more accurately, a Hell sent opportunity.

All matters presented to the Crown Court must be capable of examination by the defence and so it followed, just as the defence had their own pathologist conducting their own *post mortem*, so, the defence had their own psychologist to examine the mind of Robert Napper.

Acting for the defence was Dr Joseph, who was not only a consultant forensic psychiatrist but also a barrister at law. Prior to the interview which was conducted at HMP Belmarsh Dr Joseph had access to the police interviews and statements, he was aware that Napper had been charged with two counts of murder and rape. Napper opened up. He described his childhood as being very happy and that he was brought up in Kent. It was after his parents divorced when he was aged 12 and he moved to south east London his fortunes changed. This was demonstrated by a government plot to extend the years by doubling them. That plot resulted in the years 1973, 1975, 1977, 1979 and 1980 all being twice as long as they should have been. The result was the theft of his childhood. After leaving school and whilst working in a wine bar he met the queen on two occasions. She spoke to him about a charity event which had not gone according to plan and expected him to apologise for it.

He had no idea why the police had arrested him, he did not know any of the victims and he had never been inside 1a Heathfield Terrace so could not explain how his fingerprints were found there. During the interview with Dr Joseph he expressed a number of delusional ideas. Ideas which he himself admitted must sound unusual. He tried to either conceal these delusions or normalise them. Apart from the calendar changes and meeting the queen he also believed he was the holder of a Nobel Peace Prize. In the past he had been hunted by the IRA who had at some point captured and knee-capped him. He had been poisoned on a number of occasions and people were generally talking about him in a derogatory manner.

Throughout the interview Napper was polite and answered questions carefully. However, his use of language was abnormal and his use of grammar was incongruous. He often referred to himself in the third person (A trait associated with psychotic illness). The conclusions were that the fitness of Napper to stand trial was in doubt. Dr Joseph diagnosed him as suffering from paranoid schizophrenia, characterised by delusions of a paranoid, grandiose and possibly sexual nature, thought disorder and possible hallucinatory experiences.

Napper understood the nature of the charges and difference between guilty and not guilty, however his ability to communicate effectively with his legal advisers was affected by his susceptibility to delusions. His ability to stand trial was seriously compromised by his mental illness. Under cross-examination his explanations for events would appear ridiculous as the jury would be unaware of his mental illness.

For the prosecution Dr Don Grubin also paid a visit to Napper. He found him much the same. Napper repeated many of the same delusions almost verbatim. He would not be drawn on the offences only declaring his intent to plead not guilty. His strange pattern of talk and unusual use of words was again noted, often referring to himself in the third person. Dr Grubin concluded that Napper was suffering either from a form of Asperger's syndrome or a schizoid personality disorder. He was likely to view women as objects rather than as human beings, objects that were unobtainable to him. This together with his obsessional fantasies and isolation could drive him to sexually-motivated murder. However, in spite of his mentally-disordered state Napper should be able to defend himself in court with the assistance of legal advisers. In Dr Grubin's opinion, Napper was fit to stand trial.

In essence, the defence team had produced a doctor who pronounced him unfit to stand trial and the doctor employed by the prosecution had found the opposite. The enquiry moved to a third doctor. Consultant forensic psychiatrist Dr Janet Parrot had interviewed Napper on eight occasions over a period from 21st June 1994 to 14th February 1995. She too noted his curious manner of speech and delusional beliefs. Also that he had been referred to the Maudsley Hospital when still a child aged 13 in 1979. He had been identified as being withdrawn and depressed. This had followed the traumatic break-up of his parent's marriage and displays of violence at home.

Napper was referred again in 1989 to the Maudsley Hospital, this was immediately after he had attempted suicide and had reported to his mother that he had raped a woman in Plumstead. As a result of interview he was referred to a course of psychotherapy which began on the 3rd January 1991. After three sessions he voluntarily stopped attending. He said his employers would not allow him to take time off work. He was at this time employed by Serco at the old Woolwich Arsenal site. During his psychotherapy sessions he again made reference to an attack he had made on a woman. He believed people at his workplace knew about his past and were talking about him, which terrified him.

Napper had not shown any behavioural abnormalities during his remand at Belmarsh Prison with the exception of his stilted speech patterns centred on referring to himself in the third person. Napper repeated the same list of grandiose delusions. Dr Parrot formed the opinion that Napper's delusions in themselves would be unlikely to impede his comprehension of legal proceedings. He was fit to stand trial.

The defence requested another opinion and Dr Hamilton visited him at Belmarsh Prison on 16th March 1995. He trawled through the same delusions. His opinion differed slightly from his colleagues. He decided it was impossible to judge whether Napper could properly direct his counsel or follow proceedings. The instructions given by Napper were the product of an abnormal mental state. His advice was that the issue should be decided by a jury especially empanelled for the purpose under the Criminal Procedure (Insanity and Unfitness to Plead) Act 1991.

When the reports came back to the investigating team and were then studied by counsel it was felt that the job was done. Two to one were in favour out of three eminent psychologists saying that Napper was fit to attend criminal proceedings and a fourth saying it should be decided by a jury. On one thing they were all agreed. Napper was of an extremely dangerous disposition. If only it were as simple as a vote.

As the trial date approached, both prosecution and defence counsel were concerned with the issue of Napper's ability to stand trial. It was decided to go through all of the tests again. This time it was conducted at Broadmoor Special Hospital where it was hoped Napper may have responded to treatment. If Napper he had done so it made no difference to the resultant opinions of the same doctors who were all asked to examine him again. One interesting snippet came out of Dr Janet Parrot's report. During her examination she noted that Napper he did not refer to himself so often in the third person. When asked if he could explain this Napper replied, "It was a mistake of pronouncement." And then in his stilted manner, "In order to envisage myself, maybe I think of myself from outwards. I must have taken a side step to look in." This statement bore chilling echoes of the witness who had heard what she thought were two men arguing loudly in Samantha's flat in the early hours of the morning after her death, i.e. "Leave it. I said leave it!"

The final psychiatric report was submitted by Dr Andrew Payne, a consultant forensic psychiatrist at Broadmoor. He was requested to provide the court with a medical report. Dr Payne revealed he had interviewed Napper on eight occasions in addition to studying the psychiatric notes from the Maudsley Hospital, witness statements and the reports of his colleagues. He added nothing new to the previous reports until it came to events following Napper's arrest.

Dr Payne referred to Napper's remand to Belmarsh Prison on 30th May 1994 and how when he had first been seen by a psychologist on 6th June "There was no clear sign of mental-illness." This is a small detail but it is interesting to note how Napper was capable of concealing his mental state. This was later reviewed when, throughout June and into November, he was noted talking of calendar adjustments and meeting the queen. He was referred for assessment to Broadmoor on 22nd February 1994 and it was immediately noted how his speech was over-inclusive, in the third person and full of systemised delusions. He was accepted as a patient in Broadmoor on 21st June 1994. Napper was finally officially transferred there as an in-patient on 21st June 1995 under section 48 of the Mental Health Act 1983.

Napper fitted-in well to the routine of Broadmoor Hospital. He kept himself clean and tidy but did not mingle socially with other patients, one worrying feature was his tendency to stare at female staff to the point of making them feel uncomfortable. Dr Payne concluded by saying that, in his opinion, Napper's fitness to plead in the light of his mental illness was an issue. On direct questioning he would be unlikely to include delusional responses and his intellect and understanding are sufficient for him to be regarded as "fit to plead". The upshot of this toing and froing of analysis on the fitness of Napper to stand trial can be summarised:

- He is aged 29 born in 1966, the eldest of four children in south east London.
- His father was violent and abusive and left the family for Australia in 1978.
- He was first identified as in need of mental therapy when referred to the Maudsley Hospital in 1980.
- He attended secondary school attaining one O-Level and six CSEs, leaving at 16 years. Further education up to City and Guilds in catering.
- He worked as a cook, machine operator and storekeeper and was rarely out of employment.
- He left home in 1987 and was again referred to the Maudsley Hospital in 1989 (The first rape incident reported to his mother).
- By 1991 he was regarded as having a tenuous link with reality and the psychotic process had begun.

Examples of his delusional beliefs:

1. He feels persecuted, an example being that he believed his landlady was putting urine in his tea and applied a cigarette lighter to his testicles when he was asleep.

2. A Roman Catholic sect known as the Roman Corinthian Diddycoys were working to steal his fortune.
3. He was awarded three Nobel Prizes and a degree whilst still a child.
4. The calendar has been adjusted by the government so that certain years have been repeated. This is set out in the Strategy Manual of the British Public Advisory Service. The plot has resulted in his actual age being between 41 and 47.
5. He and his family have long been targets of revenge attacks of the IRA. He has been knee-capped and visited by Bobby Sands who was disguised as a milkman.
6. He has been sent letter bombs, one of which blew off the fingers of his hand. They were restored by his father who glued them back on by inhaling the fumes of "sparklers".
7. He served as a cadet in the Angolan wars and received three war medals
8. He has an entry in *Who's Who*.
9. He has great wealth and receives "haunted" cheques from the British government. A part of his wealth was inherited but he made a great deal of money by selling his work, *The Star Wars Trilogy* to George Lucas. He wrote it when he was 13 or 14.
10. He is capable of sending messages by telepathy.
11. He has met the Queen in very "hush hush" circumstances.

It is well worth remembering that the function of the psychiatrist's examinations of Napper was to diagnose his mental-illness and establish:

(a) Whether that illness prevent him from making a rational plea.
(b) Would it be such as to allow him to plead not guilty to murder on the grounds of diminished responsibility?

The psychiatrists remit was certainly not an interrogation about the offences. This is entrenched in case law. It is recognised, as in the case of Peter Sutcliffe (The Yorkshire Ripper), who pleaded insanity and that he was told to kill women by God, that eminent, experienced psychiatrists

may be mis-led by "cunning" patients. In the Sutcliffe case he successfully hoodwinked four psychiatrists into believing he was doing God's
work when simple interrogation about the sexual nature of the crimes
would have exposed that as a lie.

It was decided that a trial would be convened to establish Napper's
fitness to stand trial for murder and rape. The date was set for 3rd October 1995.

12" or FIVE HAND WIDTHS

NOTES

84-C5   ⊙⚊   Rice shuttleshot

9930   TABLE

846B   TREE / GREEN position

Rockmount Gardens Pole Position North Reverse.

Levi Ewarp Tooth Grin or /plus Circle 5-10.

If its Hot its Mentioned.

83 5K   Trees – PATHS – GARAGES.

56 9HJ   PATHS – Tables – Trees.

R.S.P.C.B ➤ Sparkle "SKEETER"

Really Strong Plain clothes Bobby

"plain clothes Bobby"

landmark.   SUPER Reflecting

Hermans HEAD

MANTRA :   THE JEERING

I AM A REFLECTOR

Holy BIBLE   MENTAL (Psychic) VOICE Reflecting

HECKTA   "TAKE A JUMP"

MAKEPIECE   declare

Angela   "I SAY"   KILLER   FEZ BEAR MATURE

Blister Park

Auspiscion

Soddin Filthy Bitch

N ↑

Im HERE for the illegitamate fooing

OSPREY   "OOZZINNG"

Its dead Quiet

I WANT SEPP ~~Reflect~~ Reflect

Reflect or Your dead.

"Crap A ..."

More of Napper's perplexing doodlings.

CHAPTER 32

Tragedy at the Trial

By October 1995 most of the Bisset enquiry team had been returned to either their respective divisions or, in the case of most of the detectives, had moved on to other murder enquiries. By August, virtually all the remaining team were sent back to other work. The top floor at New Scotland Yard still did not seem to appreciate the historical significance of this extraordinary enquiry and now someone was "on the sheet" (a euphemism for being charged) the case quickly slipped from notice. Press interest again had withered away.

DI Bryan Reeve had taken up a post as the detective inspector at the child protection team at Hither Green, although he continued hands on and frequently visited the incident room at Belvedere. Alan continued writing the updates to the murder report and submitted it through Bryan. It was a lonely furrow at Belvedere but at least there was plenty of space to spread out wall maps and diagrams. By the end of August even Roger and Peter Canavan had been sent back to assist in other murder investigations. Only Alan, Christine Smith and their assistant PC Rick Davey remained. Christine and Rick had their work cut out compiling the charts for court readiness. Alan was there to accede to the demands of prosecuting counsel and update police reports as well as completing any final outstanding actions.

After a few delays to the start date to the trial in November 1995, Peter and Roger returned to Belvedere to assist in the preparation for the forthcoming trial. Roger was appointed full time disclosure officer and prepared the documents, exhibits and charts ready for defence perusal. A mammoth task. At the preliminary hearing on 16th December 1994 then another on 27th February 1995 attempts were made by the defence to "split" the indictment. This is a common ploy by the defence, its object being to prevent one case, i.e. here the rape series, from "contaminating" the other with a bias; seen by many police officers as cynical, but in reality a worthwhile endeavour to dilute the prosecution case. In any event the application did not work and the trial date was set for 3rd October 1995. Meanwhile Colin Stagg continued to try and rebuild his life having returned to his flat in Roehampton. He was finding it increasingly difficult, hounded by the press, at best ignored by neighbours, at worst openly reviled.

An internal review had been started into the investigation and a second investigation had also been started into the murder. The second investigation made no link to the possibility of Napper as a suspect and Alan's small team at Belvedere received no enquiry from them. The internal enquiry found that the initial investigation into the Nickell murder had cost £3,000,000, an investment which was only to achieve lasting embarrassment to the organization. The Criminal Injuries Compensation Authority awarded Rachel's son Alex the sum of £22,000; a figure which produced the expected reaction from the press who immediately compared it to the expected handout from the MPS to Colin Stagg who remained the constant victim of suspicion and innuendo. The comparably small handout was in fact the maximum that could be awarded. Something completely different from litigation.

The *News of the World* "helpfully" paid for Colin Stagg to take a lie detector test which he passed with flying colours during a TV broadcast. It merely polarised opinion on the value of lie detectors. Those who still believed in his guilt scoffed at a device which was not accepted for use in English law. This camp tended to be the same people who had vigorously pushed the use of the new science of psychological profiling to its limit and beyond. For Colin Stagg it was trial by media, never a very self-confident person he found himself unemployable. In effect Colin Stagg was another victim of Napper. Encouraged by the press he was ostracised after his acquittal. He was shouted at and spat upon in the streets and obscenities were scrawled on his front door.

In the meantime the undercover officer Lizzie James retired from the police early and sued the force for serious psychological injury. The case was settled out-of-court for an undisclosed sum, but in any calculation far more than that received by Alex Nickell. A decision which underlined the curious feeling that "psychobabble" is alive and well and can be adapted to suit any situation.

Alan remained in contact with Margaret and Jack Morrison keeping them updated as the trial approached. Margaret was suffering and two weeks before the date set for the trial Jack took her away on a holiday to Sorrento, Italy. Margaret was dreading the forthcoming trial but had vehemently vowed her intention to be present. The holiday in Sorrento was not a success. She had been there previously with Samantha and the trip gave rise to many poignant and painful memories. Roger looked after the interests of Cosy, meeting-up occasionally. Cosy was a man who kept his emotions on a tight rein, he had been hitting the bottle since his loss and it would be a long haul for him to really start his recovery.

The detective's curse is paperwork and yet nothing is quite as onerous or as important as preparation for trial. Every detail was gone over-and-over. Information had reached Belvedere by now that William Clegg was to be the lead for the defence. This news drove all to greater efforts to try and foresee what Clegg might find as a weakness. For a successful prosecution a good detective will always be thinking "defence". "What would I go for if I were defending? Where are the weak links? Where might the case be exposed?"

Thoughts would jump into Alan and Roger's minds and discussions went on as they endlessly mulled over the case. William Clegg had a fearsome reputation as a defence lawyer. This reputation had only been enhanced by his skewering of the prosecution in the Rachel Nickell case. Alan had never come up against Clegg before and he rehearsed over and over his part in the prosecution. He didn't want to be another one of Clegg's celebrated stories of police failure. Alan steadied himself. He reminded himself of something he had always borne in mind. "Do your job to the best of your ability and you will be able to hold your own with anyone." William Clegg was, at the end of the day, just another bloke. Even so Clegg came with a certain notoriety. In any court case the police must be well prepared, or disaster will surely strike. Certain names, however, carry the day and Clegg's was one of those. Understated, fair, but relentless. There are other defence barristers, perhaps more in the public eye, whose names can raise a smile amongst police officers because their actual success in court does not quite match their celebrity. The name Clegg will provoke more of a beetled brow on the waiting lamb.

Alan's part in the investigation, as far as his court appearance, centred on being the arresting officer. Napper had made an unsolicited comment just after his arrest. There are strict rules under the Police and Criminal Evidence Act (PACE) governing when a person might be questioned or when he or she might be interviewed. Any comments outside these parameters can be ruled inadmissible. Before the introduction of PACE there had been many cases where the police relied heavily on written confessions. Many of these were disputed subsequently. The system without doubt had been abused by a small section of the police bringing the whole process into disrepute. Alan had cut his detective teeth during those days when suspects were interviewed without legal representation, and questions and answers were written in long hand. At the end of the interview the script was read over to the accused, who was then asked to initial each answer and sign at the end if their statement was correct. If the defendant refused to sign the officer would sign it and endorse the document "Refused to sign." These documents, amazingly, were still valid and would be used in court. PACE ended all that with tape-recorded interviews.

The unsolicited comment Napper had made to Alan meant that his comment was not the result of a question and was therefore valid to be noted and used. In his comment Napper had plainly said he had never been to the murder scene and did not know where it was. Alan had noted it by writing it down almost immediately and had read out the comment again to the custody officer. Napper agreed he had said it and signed the note. He again admitted to saying he had never been to Heathfield Terrace in his interview. Napper had a problem in that his fingerprints were at the scene. By saying he had never been there he negated any possible defence of ever having visited the flat legitimately and leaving his prints in the normal course of events prior to the murder.

Naturally, there were concerns about Napper's sanity. The defence could say he had been at the flat but because of his mind's disturbance had forgotten, or he had burgled the property on a previous occasion and was loathe to admit that fact to police. The fingerprints were not in blood. Added to the almost calamitous confusion between the similarity of Samantha's fingerprints and his, this was fertile ground for Mr Clegg to sow seeds of doubt.

The other evidence against Napper wasn't as watertight as the investigating team had hoped to make it such as the Adidas shoeprint in blood. The composite had been estimated by an expert as size 7 to 9. Napper took size 9. There was no shoe recovered from Napper's flat which matched the shoeprint. But there was an empty shoe box for the right type of training shoe size 9 and a receipt in Napper's name showing they had been purchased by him. Hours were spent revisiting shoeprint experts until it was established that shoeprints are very difficult to "size" and the composite could easily have been a size 9. But the original estimate had to be disclosed to the defence. Without the original trainers the defence would concentrate the jury's minds on the expert's original estimate of the shoe size being only a 7. Something Napper could not possibly wear.

The *A to Z* books, as fascinating as they might be, could be explained away as showing diagrams of running routes which naturally criss-crossed the scenes of crime as they were concentrated in a small area close to his home address. Napper's isolated and peculiar behaviour could never be relied upon as an indicator of guilt of such a heinous offence. Lessons from the Colin Stagg investigation and trial were still raw. Paul Britton could not be seriously considered a witness in the Napper case, in any event his input had been much less than in the Rachel Nickell investigation. The Bisset team were now glad of Micky Banks' scepticism of offender profiling and his view of how it was useful only up to a point. But that point should never be allowed to lead the investigation. The profile was a useful tool, an indicator and no more.

On the days leading up to the trial, boxes of paperwork and exhibits were transferred from Belvedere to the Old Bailey in readiness. Alan was totally immersed in the preparation, constantly going over-and-over in his mind avenues the defence may take. There was a short list of other suspects which had been considered, all had been eliminated satisfactorily, another list of other similar offences also loomed, although by the crime's very nature this was short. In any event the only reasonably like offence was that of Rachel Nickell. Alan assumed that as William Clegg had successfully defended Stagg in that case he would hardly now point his own client, Napper in that direction. The list of other suspects had been well bottomed-out, but there could always be an unknown thrown into the mix by the defence just to spread doubt or inference of incompetence.

Roger had just left the office on his way with exhibits on the day before the trial when Alan's pager bleeped. It was Jack Morrison. Alan used the office telephone to call Jack who was in Scotland. Believing Jack just wanted reassurance for the impending trial Alan answered cheerily, "Hello Jack. How are you? We are ready for tomorrow, I will see you and Margaret at the Old Bailey about lunchtime. There will be no rush for you to get there." There was a pause and then Jack's voice came over very quietly, his Scottish accent accentuated.

"Alan, Maggie died yesterday. Just after we got off the plane from Italy."

Alan held the phone in both hands. He sat down in the empty office.

"I am so sorry Jack."

The words felt stupid, useless.

"Aye, she was never right after what happened. She just collapsed at home after we got back from holiday and that was it."

"Jack. Will you be okay. Is there anyone there?"

"My family has gathered round. It's all a bit of a shock."

Alan looked upwards at the nicotine stained ceiling.

"Jack don't worry about this end, I will sort everything out, and naturally I will keep you informed of what's going on."

Again a silence.

"Thanks Alan. You've been a good friend and I know Maggie would appreciate it."

Another pause.

"Well I'd better get on."

"I'm so very sorry Jack. Goodbye."

Alan waited until he heard the click of the phone going down at the other end. He shuffled a few papers on his desk then looked up at the photograph of Samantha on the office wall smiling down on him, holding

Jazmine. It was the old police appeal poster. Beneath the photograph was printed in bold capitals.

DID YOU KNOW SAMANTHA BISSET?
DO YOU KNOW WHO COULD HAVE KILLED HER
AND HER 4 YEAR OLD JAZMINE?
CAN YOU HELP?

This case had taken its toll, Alan felt a tremendous sadness. Even in his own family life, although he had taken care to keep most of the facts from them he felt the effect. Two years had passed since that call to go to Thamesmead. He hadn't had much of a break since and any break he had was consumed with this case. He was a walking encyclopaedia of the life and death of Samantha Bisset. Not an evening passed without it being in the forefront of his thoughts. On every holiday he had with him notes and research work, a notebook ready to jot down any random thoughts that may pop into his head which he could pursue when he returned to the office.

Whichever way the trial went he had had enough. He realised he needed a break from it and had applied to leave the murder team. As a sort of antidote he had applied for a post in the child protection team. He felt that working for the cause of mistreated children might go some way to erase the vision of Jazmine's angelic blue lips. Child protection was seen as the least desirable of all detective work, and without much preamble he was selected and posted to start at Shooters Hill immediately after the trial.

The day of the trial arrived and best suits were to be worn, Alan wore his lucky tie, one from his Royal Navy days signifying his part in the Beira patrols off Mozambique. He had informed Bryan Reeve and Micky Banks of the tragedy of Margaret Morrison. It was with sombreness added to the usual pre-trial nerves that the team gathered in the police room and chatted over mugs of tea. The trial was to be heard in No. 1 Court. Mr Justice Hooper was designated to oversee it.

After a second mug of tea, all moved down to the main body of the courts. The Old Bailey is an intimidating structure, with vast ballroom-sized hallways which lead off to the labyrinth of courtrooms. No. 1 Court is situated at the very end, almost tucked away. Outside the courtroom, heavy wooden benches are provided for those with a long wait, giving a view of the double doors to the court with their polished brass handles and brass plate, "Number One Court", infilled with red.

From these doors an usher will appear dressed in a black gown to call the witnesses. As they go into the double doors they quickly pass through another door which shields the courtroom from any peering eyes, to those left behind it is as though they are being swallowed-up. The team gathered around one of the heavy benches as John Pearse arrived. He hadn't joined the crew for tea. Micky Banks hid it well, but there was obviously friction between them and they hardly spoke.

The trial had commenced; a jury had been sworn-in to hear the evidence of Napper's fitness to plead. This was only the first hurdle, the trial proper had not even started. If the jury decided that Napper was fit to stand trial then a new jury, who had no knowledge of the mental fitness trial, would then be sworn in for the trial proper.

Normally during these long waits outside court Alan filled in his time reading and re-reading his statement. There were at this stage no other witnesses to worry about and put at their ease. Alan's *Daily Telegraph* cryptic crossword, normally a saviour at these times, remained unstarted in the all pervading nervous atmosphere.

CHAPTER 33

A Surprise Verdict

A sudden kerfuffle and the doors to No. 1 Court swung open and people began pouring out. All those waiting on the benches outside the courtroom rose to their feet in unison. Faces were scanned of those emerging and eventually a familiar one was alighted upon. "Guilty, he's pleaded to manslaughter."

It is worth making a mention of what this means. A charge of murder can be reduced to one of manslaughter rendering the defendant not guilty of murder. This can occur by virtue of using the defence of diminished responsibility under the Mental Health Act 1957. A defence only open where there is a murder charge (not even attempted murder or, e.g. rape). It comes into effect if, although responsible for the death of another, the accused's mental state was such that, at the time of the killing, it substantially diminished his or her responsibility for their actions. Interestingly this does not include if their illness is simply a product of a psychopathic personality disorder. The burden is on the defence to establish diminished responsibility (unless, of course, as in Robert Napper's case, the prosecution agrees to accept such a plea without the need to hear the defence's full case in open court and the judge does not intervene). If successful, a verdict of not guilty to murder but guilty to the lesser offence of manslaughter will be recorded. William Clegg had obviously got through sufficiently to Napper to get him to glimpse his own madness. He must also have then admitted the rapes.

It took a few moments for this to sink in. The first reaction was relief. Now no more concerns about giving evidence. The second was a rush of pleasure. At last, after two years, this case could be put to bed. Sometimes, after the ending of a case there is euphoria, pent up emotions expelled in the nearest public house. Alan could not feel any great sense of achievement. He thought, "Must tell Jack and Margaret." Then the realisation, Margaret was dead. Another victim of the madness of the unfortunate Robert Napper. After the initial unseemly rush, counsel began to appear, both sides walking out of court together. Nigel Sweeney and David Spens made their way over and congratulated Micky Banks. David Spens was like a man with a great weight lifted from his shoulders. He was constantly smiling, he shook hands with Alan. "Well done sergeant, the world is a safer place. Sentencing will be on 9th October, just four days."

Alan smiled back. "I suppose the rape of Julia will remain on the file"

This was in reference to the first in the rape series.

"Yes I am afraid so, at least it will not affect the sentence."

Alan collected his files together and stuffed them with the unread *Daily Telegraph* into his brief case. Roger came up and said, "We are going over the road for a beer to celebrate."

Alan looked around. There was a group of those heavily involved in the enquiry, they seemed to be heading for the door. Micky Banks stood to one side talking to Bryan Reeves. "Are you coming over for a drink Guv?" Micky Banks looked-up. He looked exhausted. Shaking his head he said, "No thanks Al. I'll give it a miss."

Alan was shocked. He had never known Micky Banks turn down an invitation to a drink, if anything he would lead the way. Micky walked-off and down the vast stone stairway. Alan looked quizzically at Bryan who said, "He says he doesn't feel comfortable drinking with some people. But don't let that put you off buying me a pint." The pub was crammed with officers from the Bisset and Eccleston squads. A whip for a round of drinks had already been called and the sound of laughter greeted Bryan and Alan as they entered the pub. Roger came over with pints for both of them.

"Wow, what a turn up. No-one was quite expecting that."

Alan took a long sip. "Yeah, I still can't quite believe it. Sentencing in a few days then after the weekend I start on the child protection team." Roger looked pensive, "I still don't see why you want to do that, bloody hand-holding and mixing with Social Services, not my idea of police work."

Roger looked at his watch. "I'd better phone Cosy." He handed Alan his pint as the bar was packed solid. "Hold this mate."

There was a public telephone in the corner of the bar next to the exit. Roger elbowed his way over to it and picked up the receiver, then jamming an index finger into the ear not connected to the receiver he dialed Cosy's number. The phone was answered almost immediately by Cosy himself, who had been waiting at his parent's house for news.

"Hello Cosy, its Roger."

Before Roger could progress further a hand reached over his shoulder and slapped down the receiver cradle, cutting him off.

Roger spun round, the useless phone in hand.

"What the?"

Pearse stood inches away.

"Who are you phoning?"

"What do you mean?"

"It had better not be the press," cautioned Pearse.

Roger was aghast. "It so happens I was phoning Samantha's boyfriend to give him the result. I was speaking to him when you cut me off." Pearse stood back, slightly mollified. "I just don't want any leaks."

Roger looked at the apparently dejected DI. "I am sure you don't Guvnor, but don't you think if anyone off the Bisset team was going to do that they would have done it already?"

Pearse quietly apologised.

Roger redialed the number and relayed the happy news to Cosy. Afterwards he told Alan what had happened.

"Sweet Jesus."

Alan finished his pint, and said, "I'm off Rog. I'll see you in the morning at Belvedere." As he walked-out of the pub he half expected to see someone following him to see if he was going to Fleet Street. He made his way to Blackfriars tube station and for the first time in a long time went home early and called Jack from there to tell him the news. Jack responded in his easy quiet way and thanked Alan. His thanks didn't make Alan feel any better; it still seemed to him that because of a series of questionable decisions during the rape enquiry Jack's step-daughter and step-grand-daughter had been murdered by a man who could it now appeared have been arrested months before he killed them.

The next couple of days were spent boxing files ready for them and exhibits to be put away into storage. Another onerous but important task. Especially in this case as Alan, Roger and Bryan were feeling ever more convinced it wasn't over. Alan retained copies of anything that might assist in any future investigation. As they worked away Roger and Alan discussed not only the suspicions they had over the Rachel Nickell murder but any others Napper may have committed. There was a long gap of no known offences between the murder of Rachel on 15th July 1992 and the murders of Jazmine and Samantha on 3rd November 1993. After the sequence of rapes between which there were very short intervals, it seemed inconceivable that he would not have struck again in an intervening period of 14 months. Subsequent to that rape, Napper had stalked Paula Storey on 19th August 1992 a month after Rachel's murder and was probably stalking the young lady from Eltham who had her gym fitness card stolen on 22nd September 1992.

As mentioned before, a firearm was recovered buried on Winns Common in a biscuit tin on 19th February 1993. It was later found to have Nappers fingerprints on it after his arrest when it was re-examined. It is not known when Napper buried the tin. On 31st July 1993 (four months before the Bisset murders) Napper was stopped as a Peeping Tom in very suspicious circumstances spying on a young woman in Rutherglen Road, London SE2. As can be seen, all these confirmed incidents were firmly within an area of south east London. Alan could see the dilemma the Nickell enquiry had faced. They had to their minds a strong suspect in Colin Stagg whom they believed had a pronounced (if unproven) sexual deviancy, which, if true (rather than imagined), would make him capable of a murder such as that of Rachel Nickell.

Having hung their case on Stagg matching a psychological profile, produced by an eminent profiler, how could they then consider a suspect who fell outside one of the major rafts of the profile, e.g. number 13:

The offender will live within easy walking distance of the common and will be thoroughly familiar with the common.

To countenance a suspect who lived and apparently remained 20 miles away with no connection to Wimbledon would simply undermine their whole case. On the contrary, the Wimbledon team fully believed Stagg was driven by perverted sexual desires. In time, without their intervention, whoever it was would be allowed to kill again. If Stagg did not suffer the (imagined) extremes of sexual perversity proposed and he was arrested, an innocent man would lose his liberty and the real killer would be allowed to kill again. Not an easy choice. One perhaps made impossible by placing too much stock in the psychological profile.

Suits were donned again for sentencing on the 9th October. The trial still did not attract a huge amount of publicity or press interest so there was plenty of room in court for Alan and Roger to see Robert Napper brought up from the depths into the tiny defendant's box in No. 1 Court at the Old Bailey. Napper was quiet and withdrawn, he was wearing an open-necked shirt. His acne, which was very pronounced when Alan had arrested him, was now almost clear. His short brown hair was still parted to one side and he was still the image of the Green Chain Photofit. Without more ado, Mr Justice Hooper pronounced sentence. Napper stared straight ahead, his watery blue eyes unfocused, a look of slight bewilderment on his face.

To the first rape in her home of Julia Henly a plea of not guilty was accepted. To two attempted rapes and one rape Napper entered a plea of guilty. To the murders of Jazmine and Samantha Bisset he pleaded guilty to manslaughter. On all counts he was sentenced to a restriction order and to be detained in Broadmoor Special Hospital without limit of time. The order was made under sections 37 and 41 of the Mental Health Act 1983. Without comment Napper took one last look at the open court, he caught Alan's eye, turned and disappeared down the steps. It was truly over.

Outside the court it was a much more dignified gathering than when the news had broken of his plea. Alan saw William Clegg, still wearing wig and gown quietly chatting to a colleague. The most noticeable

feature was his twinkling eyes set in a kindly face, those of an affection-
ate uncle thought Alan. Although they were about the same age Clegg
was portly but appeared light on his feet. Alan continued to study the
man, as he did so the desire to talk to him became overwhelming. He
wanted to know did William Clegg as the defender of both Stagg and
Napper have any views on the possibility of Napper being responsible
for the Nickell murder.

How had the final interview gone between Clegg and his client Napper
when Napper finally decided to admit to the rapes and murders after such
consistently strong denials? Such thoughts in practice were wildly inappropriate and, as far as Alan knew, probably beyond any ethical boundary.
Still, it niggled, he watched Clegg, he appeared to be an approachable
man, the worst thing to happen would be a flea in his ear and a snotty
report to New Scotland Yard. It was now or never. Alan took a breath.

Just then Clegg's attention was taken by another barrister, he spun on
his heel and strode off. The opportunity had passed. Alan cursed himself
under his breath for his lack of courage and going against instinct. He
was sure Clegg had something to impart and he had cravenly fallen into
the trap of seeing the gown, not the man.

The day after sentencing Alan and Roger were at Belvedere, boxing
files, clearing desks and in a final act of closing down a job cleaning-off
the white boards. The end of 1995 was fast approaching. It was their last
day at Belvedere, Roger pounced on Alan as soon as he came into the
office. "I've just been talking to Christine."

Alan looked round, Christine was not at her desk.

He looked quizzically at Roger. "So?"

"She is really embarrassed. "

"About what?"

"She was out with Pearsey last night. They had been invited by Nigel
Sweeney's team for a post-trial dinner."

Alan's eyes widened in disbelief as Roger continued. "She expected us
to be there and Pearse told her that he had tried to get hold of us but it
was such short notice he couldn't find us." Alan laughed, "Yeah right."

"Anyway Christine sat through the meal feeling rather awkward. She
feels really embarrassed."

"Nothing to do with her Rog. I never received a message, did you?"

Roger was chuckling, "No. What do you think?"

"I just wonder what he found to talk about, I wonder if he brought up the 'Not over six foot' theory and how he was convinced in his own mind right up to the DNA result that Napper wasn't responsible for the Green Chain Walk rapes." Roger smiled ruefully. "Ah well, better get these exhibits put away."

The following Monday Roger went back to another murder investigation and Alan pitched up at the child protection team (CPT) office which was based in the Edwardian police station which sat on Shooters Hill. Parts of the old building went back to Victorian times. It sat on the same crossroads where in the late eighteenth century a gibbet marked the road to Dover out of London. The gibbet was there to contain the rotting remains of unsuccessful highwaymen who haunted the steep hill to rob travellers as they slogged up to the peak.

The work was a dramatic change from murder investigation, as Alan quickly discovered, but it was far from the quiet life. The caseload per officer was at a dangerously high level. Later when computers were introduced it was plain to see by a quick cross-reference that the Shooters Hill office had the heaviest caseload in London. It covered Greenwich, Bexleyheath, Thamesmead, Eltham, Sidcup and Slade Green. These boroughs contained some of the most deprived housing estates in the country, although it was soon made apparent that class and social standing was no indicator of the potential for sexual abuse against children.

The worst and most obvious constriction was the severe curtailment of allowed overtime. The office was incredibly cramped and at times needed "hot desking". Within a short period of time it became obvious to Alan that the CID command gave little thought and certainly no kudos to these outposts of important detective work. At least Alan had an ally knowing that Bryan Reeve was running a CPT office in an adjacent Borough.

The second day at Shooters Hill and Alan made his way up the narrow stairs to the second floor. The door was open and there was the usual busy buzz of phones ringing and the chatter of officers talking. Alan was suddenly met at the doorway by the office clerk, Geordie. He looked put out. "Where have you been? The guvnor's been looking for you." Alan made a point of looking at his watch. "Eight-thirty start, its not 25 past yet."

Geordie turned towards the detective inspector's office, indicating Alan should follow. The office fell into a hushed silence and all eyes turned towards Alan. Tom Simmons a detective constable who was to become a firm friend stood up from behind his desk and grabbed Alan's arm. "The assistant commissioner has been on the blower asking for you."

Alan looked up as the others nodded.

Alan thought, "Bloody Hell," but said, "Thanks Tom, prepare my leaving do will you?" Alan followed Geordie down through the main office stopping at the door to DI Dave Allen's spacious lair (in comparison to the cheek by jowl confinement of the factory floor). Geordie unnecessarily tapped on the door and announced Alan's arrival. DI Allen looked up. "Thank you Geordie." Geordie departed leaving a space for Alan to enter. Dave Allen smiled, but not too warmly.

"Mr Johnstone has called twice, he has asked to speak to you and chooses not to say what it is about. Any ideas?"

"Not a clue Guvnor."

Alan could understand Dave Allen's concern. The highest ranking officer to have visited the office in months was the area detective chief inspector and even he was rarely seen. Now the assistant commissioner was making personal telephone calls.

"Well here's his number, you'd better use my phone, there'll be no privacy out there." He pointed vaguely toward the hubbub beyond his door, then shoved a handwritten number across the desk. Alan noted he made no attempt to leave. He turned the telephone around and dialed the number. After a couple of rings it was answered. Alan was expecting the call to go through to a secretary or whatever assistant commissioners use to fend off callers. "Ian Johnstone" came the clear response.

"Good morning sir, DC Jackaman here." The temporary rank of detective sergeant had been left behind with the box files at Belvedere.

"Thanks for getting back to me." Alan felt heartened, this was definitely not going to be a rollicking.

Ian Johnstone continued, "I need you to do a job for me. Are you able to fly to Scotland on Friday?" "Yes sir, that shouldn't be a problem."

"I have been informed that the mother of Samantha Bisset is having her funeral on Saturday and the family have requested that you attend."

Alan was surprised that suddenly the backwater job had reached such dizzying importance. "I can certainly do that sir." "Okay. Good, make all your own arrangements for travel, any problems whatsoever refer them back to me."

Alan's mind raced, he couldn't resist. "I am scheduled a rest day on Saturday and Sunday, naturally I can cancel them if authorised." May as well get authority from the top if there was overtime to be had.

"You will be representing the service. Do whatever is necessary."

Alan looked up at DI Allen who had followed the mention of over-time with interest.

"Yes sir. I understand."

"By the way, that was a good job you did on the Bisset enquiry, well done."

"Thank you sir."

The phone clicked and Alan handed the receiver back to Dave Allen who replaced it in its cradle.

"So what's that about?"

"Just tidying up on the last job I worked on. I've got to go up to Scotland on Friday. I am afraid I will have to cancel my weekly leaves on Saturday and Sunday. Too bad but that is with less than eight days notice."

"I got that bit," Allen replied.

"Pity, but can't be helped. I am representing the service apparently."

And so, on the Friday, Alan found himself flying north, back to Aberdeen, no doubt as a pawn in someone else's giant game of chess. But the opportunity had arisen for him to pay his last respects to Margaret and to personally offer his condolences to Jack. The funeral was scheduled to take place in Dundee and on a drizzly cold morning Alan attended it at Barnhill cemetery, the same as where Samantha and Jazmine were buried. Afterwards at the reception he spent some time with Jack who introduced him to many of his family. Jack was stoic about the tragic events which had piled-up on him. He confided that he did feel bitterness that the rape enquiry had, seemingly he felt through its apparent mismanagement, allowed Robert Napper his freedom to murder Margaret's beloved Samantha and Jazmine. Alan nodded his sympathy without going into the errors of the enquiry. It wasn't the place or the time. Jack asked Alan to stay in touch and come and visit him sometime at his beautiful house at Craster.

On Sunday morning Alan made his way back down to London. He had had time to reflect on the events of the past two years. He could not get the image of Jazmine's blue lips out of his head. Then, the marking of Isabella Plantation in Napper's *A to Z*, the Photofit, the stoop and the resemblance to Colin Stagg, the horrific injuries inflicted upon both Rachel and Samantha. That curious, knowing, half smile on the avuncular face of William Clegg as he had emerged from Napper's confession to killing Samantha and Jazmine.

Something definitely wasn't right. He should be feeling content after such a struggle to convict Napper, but, still, the voice within him gnawed away. He would telephone Roger in the morning.

CHAPTER 34

The Long Haul

Roger and Alan met up to talk through events. A strategy was needed to keep the job alive. There was certainly no appetite within the Metropolitan Police Service to keep the enquiry going. There was more of a feeling that it would deal with the fallout of the Stagg trial as quickly and quietly as possible. Between them they decided to meet up regularly to discuss any updates and any ideas of carrying the case forward. It was definitely going to be an uphill struggle with no formal backing whatsoever.

The feeling remained strong that if they stuck at it something would turn-up. Rather like the astrophysicist Paul Murdin who had been given the opportunity to discover the theory of the existence of black holes. Something that nobody could see, but he went on to prove they were there. Just because Colin Stagg had been found not guilty of the murder of Rachel Nickell this did not mean he was automatically entitled to any financial compensation. After the trial and conviction of Napper there was a brief surge of renewed interest from the press. Most of the nationals gave the story some prominence although not front page. Not yet. Such headlines included:

"SEX ATTACKER ADMITS SAVAGE KILLING OF MOTHER AND GIRL, 4"— *The Times* 10/10/95

"MOTHER AND CHILD STALKED AND KILLED BY SCHIZOPHRENIC"— *The Telegraph* 10/10/95

"DOUBLE KILLER SENT TO BROADMOOR"—*The Guardian* 10/10/95

Of far more concern to the MPS were the leaders in:

The Daily Mail—"DID HE KILL RACHEL TOO?"

The Daily Express—"SEX KILLER IS FACING QUIZ OVER RACHEL."

Someone, somewhere was starting to add things up. Where the source was for such information Alan and Roger wondered, for there seemed to be no such belief within the MPS. After the initial flurry of speculation, all quietened down again. The force had suffered severe criticism over the Nickell investigation and decisions were made to mitigate and repair this. After the acquittal of Colin Stagg a statement was issued that police were "not looking for any other person" in connection with the murder of Rachel Nickell although the investigation remained open. This is code for the benefit of the media to interpret, i.e. "The court was mistaken and Colin Stagg did it." This misplaced innuendo had the effect of inflaming media prejudice against not only Colin Stagg but Mr Justice Harry Ognall too.

The internal review of the Nickell investigation was concluded in November 1994. Its findings were that circumstantial evidence of Colin Stagg being the murderer existed in fact, but the evidence was "inconclusive". Hardly a ringing endorsement of Stagg's innocence. Out of the review came a recommendation to set up a new enquiry team which was duly formed under the command of Detective Superintendent Peter Charnley. The remit of the re-investigation was not to start from scratch but to continue on from the original with a fresh approach. They were told to keep an open mind as to the identity of the killer. Their enquiry did include a discussion with Micky Banks over the possibility of Napper being responsible for the murder of Rachel Nickell. No other members of the Bisset team were interviewed, least of all Roger and Alan who went blissfully unaware that another investigation was even under way.

The new investigation interviewed Napper at Broadmoor Hospital on 20th December 1995, an interview which was, somewhat bizarrely to Alan's thinking, undertaken by DI John Pearse and was classified as a "post-conviction interview". A much later review expressed surprise at the choice of interviewer but conceded Pearse had in fact managed to engender some rapport with Napper. The interview did not result in any further admissions.

Napper was asked about the Rachel Nickell murder and he held out an alibi that he was at work at Serco on the other side of London in Woolwich at the time. The work records having been destroyed, checks were made with his ex-colleagues and managers who by the best of their recollection agreed Napper had been working a normal day shift on the 15th July 1992, the date of the murder, making it impossible for him to have been in Wimbledon at 10 am on the morning of the murder. That was enough for the investigation to lose interest in Napper.

The second investigation culminated in a written report by Detective Superintendent Tomkins which was submitted in May 1998. The conclusion was that no further suspect had been identified. The dust was settling, Alan, Roger and Bryan had other jobs to concentrate on but every few months they would meet up for a discussion. By 1998 the consensus was that the cards had been finally dealt and it was hard to convince the press other than that (heavily paraphrased):

(a) Colin Stagg was guilty.
(b) Mr Justice Harry Ognall had been hoodwinked by legal tomfoolery and wasn't fit to serve as a judge.
(c) Paul Britton had been discredited.

These themes were carried on relentlessly, in a manner which only the British national press can pursue with determined vigour, blithely ignoring the facts in a kind of sickening self-righteousness formerly reserved for the Spanish Inquisition.

By the end of 1998 two things occurred which changed the trajectory of the unofficial investigation into whether or not Napper had murdered Rachel Nickell. The first was the publication by Paul Britton of his book

The Jigsaw Man. The book, notably, made no direct connection between the Nickell and Bisset murders. The second was far further down the list of national importance. Alan eventually passed the arcane assessment centre procedure and was selected to become a sergeant, an event which caused him to be transferred back to the murder team as a detective sergeant. It also revitalised his interest in the investigation of homicide. He joined a team under Detective Chief Inspector Richard Heselden, one which went on to have a fantastic string of results in many complex and high profile cases.

Prior to his elevation to the giddy heights of detective sergeant, Alan had another boost. He was notified that he was to receive a commendation from Assistant Commissioner Ian Johnstone for his work on the Napper case. Nothing to get too egotistical about, however it did please him, prior to being promoted, to see the certificate was made out to Acting Detective Sergeant Jackaman and was for, "Leadership, Detective Ability and Victim Support in a double murder and linked series of rapes." Having tried the promotion system and failed for the past five years it was pleasing to see those words, especially "Leadership."

In August 1998 after discussion with Bryan and Roger, Alan wrote a letter to Paul Britton in which he explained his misgivings about Napper and his belief in his guilt concerning the murder of Rachel Nickell. The letter of which the following are key extracts was dated 9th August 1998. After his introduction, Alan explained his part in the Napper enquiry. To paraphrase:

"Allow me to formulate a theory I have long held that Napper may well be responsible for the murder of Rachel Nickell.

I believe you were absolutely correct in your assessment that Samantha would not have allowed this man (Napper) in. Her fiery nature and fierce protectiveness towards Jazmine was well documented and may well have been her undoing. This may be compared with the comparative submissive nature of Nappers earlier rape victims.

You will have gathered I have an enduring interest in the case of Robert Napper. There are many points of the case which are of interest to the investigator of murder and to the analysis of psychotic behaviour. I am more than willing to discuss them at length with you, should you consider it worthwhile.

The nub of my argument is, the enquiry team investigating the Rachel Nickell murder were too blinkered and fell into the classic trap of believing in the guilt of Stagg to the exclusion of all other possibilities.

When the matter of the possibility of Napper being responsible for the murder of Rachel was raised with DI Pedder his reaction was almost hostile and he dismissed this theory out of hand.

The same reaction was experienced when the idea was first floated that Napper was a very likely candidate for the Green Chain rapes. DI Pearse the deputy SIO was also adamant Napper could not have been responsible.

Protection of reputations can be a prickly issue.

Napper is now residing at a secure mental hospital, is it possible for you as a clinical psychologist to gain access to Napper with a view to asking him further questions about Rachel Nickell? I realise this will only be possible if there has been an improvement in his mental health. I understand the confidentiality of any 'Confession' which may be given. I also understand that any interview involving police if it relates to unsolved offences, must be conducted strictly within the remit of PACE."

The letter, which contained much more information than shown above, did not elicit a written response but it did lead to a series of telephone conversations. Paul Britton explained he had no power or sway over interviews conducted at Broadmoor. He was still feeling sore at his treatment at the hands of the media and the MPS whom he felt had left him on his own to face the music. He was still intrigued by the case and agreed with Alan there was a possibility of Napper being responsible for

Rachel's murder but he was loathe to be involved. The conversation was ended with that rather unsatisfactory conclusion.

When writing the letter, Alan had no idea Napper had been interviewed at Broadmoor by the "second investigation" team or by DI John Pearse.

As the millennium turned the MPS set up a new department. Initially known as the Murder Review Group (MRG), its remit was to investigate unsolved murders. Staff were recruited from officers who had recently retired, or were about to retire, and had proven in-depth experience of murder investigation. A scoping exercise was carried out by ex-Detective Chief Superintendent Albert Patrick on all unsolved murders spanning a 20 year period from 1989. The list turned-up approximately 300 outstanding, unsolved murders over this era. The outstanding murders were then dealt out to reviewing officers on the newly formed MRG whose remit was to study all the available files and report on their forensic and other potential for re-investigation. The value of the MRG was quickly realised. This innovative idea was a nationwide first and other forces began to apply to the MPS for their old cases to be reviewed. Within a few years county police forces created their own review systems, the smaller forces combining.

It was realised that the review system could be utilised to monitor current murder investigations and a system was devised termed the 28 day review. In essence, any current murder which had not charged a suspect within 28 days of the offence would be subject to a review. This initially caused some consternation amongst SIOs but was soon accepted as the experience of the reviewers was only ever used in an advisory capacity never as a wing of the complaints system. Other forces also used the facility, notably in the Soham, Cambridgeshire murder of two little girls, Holly Wells and Jessica Chapman in 2002. In such investigations as these the overview of a review was invaluable. Cambridgeshire had no in-house experience of dealing with such media exposed enquiries.

In 2000 the case of Rachel Nickell came to the top of the pile for review and was allocated to a review team based at Westminster. A painstaking analysis was made of all the potential forensic possibilities and in 2001 the result was returned from the Forensic Science Laboratory, there were no positive DNA results obtained. This outcome set alarm bells ringing with the review DCI. Surely there should at least have been a DNA result showing Rachel Nickell's own DNA.

At the closing of 2001, Alan was in serious conversation with DCI Dick Heselden. Alan was four years past his retirement date and had heard that the review team were on a recruitment drive for experienced ex-detectives. He fancied he had a chance of getting the job.

Dick faced Alan over his desk in his office at Shooters Hill. The child protection team had moved on and now all offices at Shooters Hill had been given over to the murder team. Dick was animated. "We have had such a brilliant run, Nobody can touch or even come close to our record."

Alan was relaxed in Dick Heselden's company, they had become trusted friends over the past few years, even if Heselden drove Alan mad with his insatiable appetite for taking on new jobs. Every time Dick attended a monthly meeting at area office the team would dread Dick's return. Beforehand Alan would say, "We are at absolute capacity Guv. We can't take another job." Only for Dick to bound in, "It's only a Category C, we can do this out of Book 40." This was reference to the old Metropolitan Police A4 hardback book. It meant no HOLMES account, just a handwritten record. Eyes would search heavenward and the team would roll over the job like a well-oiled machine whilst carrying on with the other, sometimes six or seven jobs they were currently handling.

Alan sipped his mug of tea. "Gotta call a stop sometime Guv."

"Yes but not now, we've had such a great sequence of results and we have just taken on another Category A."

Alan remembered a couple of things that needed doing on that job, a shooting in a pub car park on the outskirts of Croydon.

"Well, I've got to get through the interview first."

Dick looked over the desk, "Look Al, stay on here, I can guarantee to get you the next rank, DI before you finally retire."

Alan laughed. "How are you going to do that? It's not in your gift. Anyway I promised myself after the last bollocks with becoming sergeant I would never do that again. Rather a case of striving for something that's not worth having." Dick was one of those blessed souls with the ability to sail through assessment centres and examinations and had famously with ten years in the job sat the sergeants exam for the first time and come top in the MPS, consequently being selected for Bramshill Police College. This same Dick Heselden said, "Look, I will get you through that exam, I promise you."

Alan was briefly tempted but knew assessment centres were not his forte. In his view they were not centred on identifying ability, more of a race to achieve equality ending in the promotion of box ticking boors with Conformity and Timidness the gods that ruled. "Well thanks for your support Guv, but I'll give the review interview a try."

At the end of 2001 Alan attended a selection panel and was chosen to become a research officer on the MRG. On his last day at Shooters Hill in February 2002 he was working on the Croydon car park murder until 9 pm, the enquiry was at a critical stage and it was all hands to the pump. Later that evening Alan logged-off showing four hours overtime on the day he retired. He couldn't wait to restart in the MRG in six weeks time. There was a particular case he was very interested in.

During his last meeting with Roger in February 2002 he was told that a report had been leaked from Broadmoor that Napper had made more progress in his mental recovery. He was currently being assessed with a view to his release. How true this was Alan never established. It seemed there wasn't any more time to lose. After his induction into the MRG Alan was posted with others to an office in Westminster. Another Victorian survivor but with a view over the Thames and up to the minute computing systems with large modern desks.

Alan's first question naturally was, "Has the Rachel Nickell enquiry been allocated yet?" The answer was in the affirmative. Not only that, but the review team looking into it was in the same office he had been posted to at Westminster. He was directed to an office at the far end of the open plan room. The office was glass panelled and Alan knocked lightly on the door and entered. The DCI was seated at his desk and looked round quizzically. Alan introduced himself and explained he had been on the Bisset enquiry team nine years previously. He went on to explain that as a result of that murder investigation he had always fancied Robert Napper as a suspect for Rachel. The DCI adjusted his spectacles, he reached out to the pile of paperwork on his desk and produced a sheet of paper on which were a long list of names. "You can add it to the others," He said, with more than a note of weariness in his voice.

Alan was aware that his enthusiasm was not as infectious as he had believed. "Well, what I will do is write out a quick report for you outlining why I believe Napper could have done this." The DCI smiled, "Great idea." His eyes indicated where the door was.

Alan went immediately back to his new desk. He pushed aside the murder review files that had recently been given to him and began to write. The short report drew attention to the physical similarities between Napper and Stagg and the Photofits and included the stoop. The *modus operandi* of Napper of committing increasingly ever more violent attacks on women of the same age and description as Rachel ending just before Rachel's murder. The links to Wimbledon Common via the marking of Isabella Plantation in Napper's *A to Z*. The short report ended:

Conclusion

Napper is currently serving concurrent life sentences at Broadmoor where, it has been directed by the judge, that he is such a danger to the public, he serve life.

Possible lines of enquiry

Compare shoeprints found at the scene of the Nickell murder and where a suspect was seen washing himself, to the composite shoeprint of Napper's trainer print.

Compare the 'doodles' of Napper to the scene at Wimbledon to see if there are any commonalities.

Should any advances be made in identifying foreign DNA at the scene to compare it with that of Napper.

Establish through psychiatrists at Broadmoor whether nine years later Napper is fit enough to be interviewed with regard to the Nickell murder.

The report was hurriedly written and grammatically imperfect. Alan had just a limited amount of material to refer to and most of what he wrote down was from memory. As he read through the report Dickie Bird, who was seated next to him and was renowned as a bit of a wag, leaned over and said in a stage whisper, "It was Napper wot done it." This was a thinly disguised dig at the amount of times Alan had talked through his belief that Napper was responsible for Rachel's murder. The idea had stuck with Dickie, who was well-known for taking comical digs at any target. Whenever in any future enquiry Alan became excited about a suspect, Dickie would inevitably chip in "It was Napper wot done it."

Alan reflected for a moment. Was he blinded by his belief? Could it be that he had convinced himself and fallen into the old tunnel-vision trap he had accused others of? He read through the report carefully. It was all there. He just needed somebody to look at it.

He rose from his swivel chair, walked down the office and tapped on the DCI's door. The DCI again looked-up and spotted the report in Alan's hand. Alan opened the conversation.

"I've just knocked this out. There is more."

The DCI indicated an overflowing tray.

"Thanks. I'll add it to the list for elimination."

Alan never did get seconded onto the Rachel Nickell review, within a short space of time he found himself back at Shooters Hill and working in a tiny office with Albert Patrick and Terry Keating.

That same year, 2002, the DCI at Westminster asked for and was given authority for an independent forensic assessment to be carried out on the tapings and fibres from the Rachel Nickell forensic exhibits. All tests again proved negative. Around two years later, in September 2004 Alan was at his desk at Shooters Hill when he received a telephone call. It was from one of the investigators on the Nickell review. He was told that it was top secret but a foreign DNA source had been extracted from an exhibit. It was very weak and there was no possibility at the moment of identifying it, but it was promising and Napper had *not* been excluded. Alan could hardly believe it. He sat at his desk feeling numb. Could it be, after all this time? He walked through to the adjacent office where

Dickie Bird, who had followed him from Westminster to Shooters Hill, was chatting at his desk. Alan couldn't resist it.

"Dickie."

"Yeah."

"It was Napper wot done it."

Dickie Bird smiled his ruddy smile, little realising the information Alan had just been made privy to.

The maxim of a good detective had been followed by the Westminster review team DCI. Having been told by the forensic branch there were no traces of any DNA from any of the exhibits including exhibit WL4, which were vaginal and anal tapings taken at the scene, he asked himself why had they not at least shown Rachel's DNA?

Consultation was arranged with the Metropolitan Police Director of Forensic Services and a decision was made to run the tests again. This time using an alternative forensic company called LGC forensics.

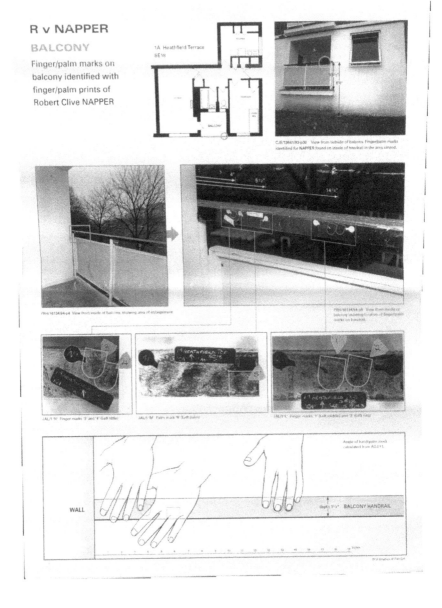

Some of the forensic evidence from Samantha Bisset's
flat as it was presented at Napper's trial.

CHAPTER 35

The Finishing Line in Sight

As in the inspired decision of Micky Banks ten years previously when he ordered the fingerprints at 1a Heathfield Terrace to be re-examined, the decision to run the DNA-tests with a different forensic provider was equally inspired. The exhibits were prioritised as the tests were long and involved. Exhibit WL4 featured half-way down the list and did not reach its turn until 2004. DNA-analysis was carried out using the technique of SGM Plus profiling and in September of 2004 the scientists hit the jackpot. Not only was Rachel's DNA-profile identified but also a tiny male component was also picked up. The male component was then cross-referenced with the list of Rachel's murder suspects. The profile did not match Colin Stagg, but it did match Robert Clive Napper.

The murder review of Rachel Nickell was transferred to a major investigation team (MIT) and changed its status from review to investigation. This had the benefit of a full team within the homicide command being given total charge of the investigation with the resultant full and prompt back-up of all other departments.

The evidence of the DNA, although it had the benefit of placing the investigation team on track, was not sufficiently strong to reach an evidential standard. The investigation team had to dig much deeper. The first point of attack was to research Napper's alibi of being at work in Serco in Woolwich at the time of the murder. Alan had reported during the investigation into the Bisset murder that after Serco had closed the records had been destroyed. Further enquiries had been unable to establish his attendance, apart from Napper's work colleagues' recollections as to whether he was working on the day in question.

Napper's run of unbelievable luck had really changed. From the time when he avoided a blood sample during the Eccleston rape enquiry to the uncanny resemblance of his fingerprints at the Bisset scene resulting in their initial elimination, just as in the Casino the bank will always win. There had been more improbable coincidences and labyrinthine changes of fortune than anything contained in the most complex of Charles Dickens or Victor Hugo novels. The twists had not ended yet.

One of Napper's erstwhile foremen from Serco was interviewed by the new investigating team. Almost as an aside he mentioned that he had kept the year planner chart of employees working hours and it was in his loft. The detectives waited with bated breath as he returned downstairs with the document. The anticipation was unbearable as the chart was opened. On 15th July 1992, the day of Rachel's murder, Napper was shown as being off work for the day.

A decision was reached that it was time Napper was re-interviewed and contact was made with Broadmoor Special Hospital. Initially the approach was rebuffed by the hospital, who felt another interview may impact on his health. It must be stressed that Broadmoor is a hospital and not a prison although it caters for some extremely dangerous patients and is secure; its primary function is for the care of its patients and it operates under the authority of the NHS.

After negotiation with the medical team, arrangements were made to enable the interview of Napper but under strict medical supervision. Despite their care for his welfare, Napper proved uncooperative and answered "No comment" to all questions. Through his solicitor he produced a prepared statement in which he denied any involvement in the murder of Rachel Nickell.

The enquiry team contacted Alan and Roger, Alan for his knowledge of the investigation into the Bisset murders and with Roger for his knowledge of all the original exhibits and their trails from the Bisset murder. The first meeting at a room in New Scotland Yard was very cordial. It was at a low level, Detective sergeant and below. At this meeting Alan was asked to attend the incident room and address the investigating team to give the benefit of his knowledge of Napper. He readily agreed and accepted the invitation, wanting to be involved as much as possible and felt he had a lot to offer.

Within a week he was to be disappointed, following a further meeting between the exhibits officer, a detective sergeant, Alan and Roger he was told that he would not be attending any team briefings. It had been decided that in the light of the sensitivity of the enquiry and the running fear of leaks to the press the SIO wanted to keep his team as tight as possible. Alan was out. The slight embarrassment as the news was imparted didn't last.

Alan could see their point. Already a reporter by the name of Stephen Wright had written an article for the *Daily Mail* which made headline news on November 9th 2004. The front page included pictures of Napper and Rachel. The headline was:

PRIME SUSPECT Face of the psychopath in Broadmoor who police believe murdered Rachel.

Again there was a constant drip feed to the press and it seemed to centre on that newspaper.

Whilst the work with the DNA-analysis continued other possible avenues were pursued. When Napper had been arrested for the Bisset murder in 1994 there was obviously keen interest in his footwear, specifically trying to find a match for the composite trainer print found in blood at Heathfield Terrace. Although the actual trainer was never found, some success was achieved with the recovery of the shoe box for an Adidas Phantom Low training shoe and the accompanying receipts for its purchase. Little attention was paid by the Bisset enquiry team to the other footwear in Napper's bed-sit, they were concentrating on Adidas Phantom Low trainers. Amongst that footwear was a pair of fairly common shoes, the pair Napper had worn on his arrest by Alan back in 1994. On Napper's conviction for the Bisset murders and subsequent referral to Broadmoor, his personal clothing and other items were restored to him. Napper's shoes from the time of his arrest for the Bisset murders were still in storage at Broadmoor. They were compared against the cast taken from next to the stream where a suspect was seen washing his hands on Wimbledon Common. It matched. When Alan had put forward his views to the review in 2002 he had mentioned that the composite trainer should be compared to a footprint found by the stream where a suspect was seen by the witness to be washing his hands. Alan was unaware that the footprints were not of a trainer but a shoe. However, once again there was dispute over the print because the size appeared to be too small. This had echoes of the Bisset enquiry when the initial sizing of the shoe was also given as too small. Further analysis was undertaken and it was proven that the print was laid down in soft ground. It was mid-summer. It had gradually dried in the sun causing shrinkage. Taking the drying into account it was a perfect match.

One more invaluable and incredible piece of evidence surfaced. After the murder of Rachel, upon examination of her son Alex, tiny fragments of unexplained flecks of red paint had been recovered from Alex' hair. One of the most obvious exhibits recovered from Napper's bedsit was a red metal toolbox which contained his books on death, the *A to Z*, knives and other incriminating items. The red paint from the box was to be compared to the paint flecks found in Alex' hair, combed out and retained. The investigators were then confronted with another dilemma. The method to compare the two paint samples was only available at Durham University and the destructiveness of the testing programme meant that it would be possible to carry out the test once only.

The decision was taken to carry out the examination and much to the team's relief it was shown there was a positive match between the two samples and that the paint was manufactured in the USA. However, the test also showed that the composition of the metal alloy attached to the samples from the box and from the flecks from Alex' hair were different. This suggested that the samples had been painted onto a different surface and it therefore followed the paint flecks were not from the same source as the toolbox. Further tests were carried out on the toolbox taking samples from different parts of it. This revealed that some parts of the box had the same metal alloy as found in the flecks from Alex' hair. This strengthened the case considerably. How the paint flecks were transferred from a heavy metal toolbox to Alex' hair may never be satisfactorily explained.

The extra evidence was all very well but further enhancement of the DNA from exhibit WL4 would be the key. The first thing to prove was that over the years there was no possibility of cross-contamination of the exhibit whilst at the laboratory. This was to rebut any future allegation that the DNA "hit" was corrupted. This exercise was time consuming and laborious but was completed to the highest degree. Whilst this was being carried out, new DNA forensic opportunities were developed which carried the forensic evidence still further.

The question was asked in February 2006, "Could the elements of the DNA-sample be used to positively eliminate Napper? Even if the match probability to implicate him could not be improved?" The answer to that question was an emphatic "Yes".

A process was developed which, as a side effect, improved technical frontiers of DNA forensic science. The end result was that the match probability to the DNA from the most intimate of scene samples to that of Robert Napper was 1: 4,000,000. The evidence was now overwhelming. The search for the truth was over.

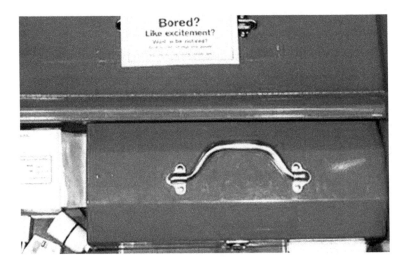

Robert Napper's red toolbox.

CHAPTER 36

A Man Awaits His End

Rather than have Napper produced to the court from Broadmoor he received formal notification of his impending trial for the murder of Rachel Nickell via a summons. This was given to him on 7th December 2007. All further court hearings up to the time of the trial were agreed by all parties to be conducted via a video link. The date of the trial was eventually set for the 18th December 2008. It was 15 years and one month since Micky Banks and his team had started their investigation into the murders of Samantha and Jazmine Bisset.

Paul Britton was charged with professional misconduct by the British Psychological Society. The charge was rightly dropped in 2002.

In January 2007 the Home Office confirmed that Colin Stagg was to be awarded £706,000 for wrongful prosecution and made a public apology to him.

The Independent Police Authority (IPCC) conducted their own investigation into the actions of the Metropolitan Police Service. The report was released on the 3rd of June 2010 and was extremely critical. They listed a catalogue of errors, bad decisions and missed opportunities which resulted in the deaths of Samantha and Jazmine Bisset.

The main criticisms were:

1. A failure to investigate the report by Napper's mother of her son's admission to the rape in Purrett Road in 1989.
2. Napper being inconceivably eliminated from enquiries into the Green Chain Walk series of rapes because he was over 6' tall.

Without these errors Napper could have been off the streets before he murdered Rachel Nickell or Samantha and Jazmine Bisset.

No disciplinary action was recommended, all key officers had since retired and the SIO of the Green Chain Walk rapes enquiry was deceased. Criminal prosecution was never a consideration.

This complex and divided investigation underlines the difficulties which may be experienced by those tasked with the investigation of serious crime. Mistakes can be made, wrong turns taken, however, these errors occur despite the best of intentions. No detective worth his salt sets out to purposefully undermine an enquiry but, unfortunately, because of the very nature of the work, poor decisions can produce catastrophic results. As an investigation grows, more outside influences come into play placing unforeseen demands and pressures on enquiry leaders and their teams. Looking back from the safety of an armchair it is easy to criticise; until one has worked in the cauldron of conflicting demands with added time constraints one should not perhaps be quick to judge.

Index

Serial Killers and the Phenomenon of Serial Murder
A Student Textbook

David Wilson, Elizabeth Yardley and Adam Lynes
Foreword by Steve Hall

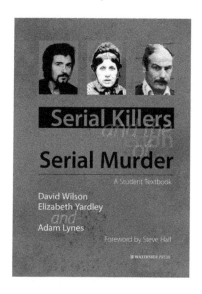

Serial Killers and the Phenomenon of Serial Murder examines and analyses some of the best known cases from English criminal history, ancient and modern. It looks at the lifestyles, backgrounds and activities of those who become serial killers and identifies clear categories of individuals into which most serial killers fall.

Paperback | ISBN 978-1-909976-21-4 | 2015 | 224 pages

www.WatersidePress.co.uk

Lightning Source UK Ltd.
Milton Keynes UK
UKHW011107120620
364903UK00002B/138